BACKS TO
THE WALL

Best wishes Chris

Enjoy the Book

Bryn

HOW HAROLD WAGSTAFF LED THE NORTHERN UNION TO ASHES VICTORY IN THE RORKE'S DRIFT TEST MATCH

A Novel based on History by
Bryn Woodworth

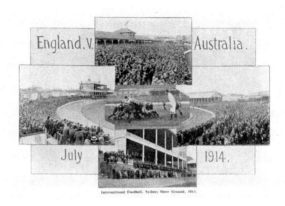

International Football, Sydney Show Ground, 1914.

Interest in the Northern Union Tour of 1914 was extremely high in Sydney. Here we see the packed Royal Agricultural Society Showground which was the venue for the first test match of the tour.

This commemorative postcard is reproduced with kind permission of the Royal Agricultural Society of NSW Heritage Centre.

CONTENTS

DEDICATION

This book is dedicated to the memory of the thirteen brave men who won the Ashes in 1914 and gave the world the Rorke's Drift Test Match.

Specifically: Alf Wood, Frank Williams, Harold Wagstaff, Billy Hall, Willie Davies, Stuart Prosser, Fred Smith, Jack Chilcott, Dick Ramsdale, Percy Coldrick, Billy Holland, Douglas Clark and Chick Johnson, heroes all.

The test match got its name when an Australian journalist compared it with the famous defensive action by the British Army during the Zulu War, where many VC's were awarded. The victory achieved by the team on the 4th July 1914 must rank as the greatest example of sporting bravery ever seen. No medals were awarded that day (or since) to the thirteen men who represented the Northern Rugby Football Union on that momentous occasion, but the metaphorical Ashes were won and brought back to a Britain that was at war.

I hope that by writing this book I have helped in a small way to preserve the memory of their great achievement and brought it to the attention of a new generation of sports fans.

Other people are also doing their bit to preserve the memory of the feats of the 1914 tourists. I am grateful to Colin Booth for drawing my attention to this celebratory event in their honour organised by Rugby League Cares.

FOREWORD

Born and bred on a council estate in Fartown, with Town Ground and Fartown each less than fifteen minutes walk away, it's hardly surprising that I grew up mad on sports. My dad and eldest brother were both rugby followers but most of my mates were Town fans. In the late fifties and early sixties the two teams seemed to have their home matches on alternate Saturdays so it was down to Leeds Road one week and Fartown the next. Entrance to Fartown was free to juniors whereas the Town matches cost a full 9 old pence (about 4p), a significant portion of my 2/6d (12 ½p) pocket money.

The first game I went to see at Fartown was an end of season testimonial match on a lovely early summer evening. The match had a feast of tries – partly due to the star players who were present and partly due to the lack of enthusiasm in the tackling. Not that I noticed or cared. I have one clear memory of the game which involved none other than the great Billy Boston. As he received the ball on the wing, round about the half-way line he had one player to beat. The defender was determined to stop him and grabbed the great man by his shorts – which he was left holding onto as Billy raced away from him and crossed the line to touch down under the posts. He was wearing a weird garment under his shorts which only partly protected his modesty. I later learned that this strange item of underwear was in fact a jock strap. The great man had a big smile on his face as he was congratulated by his team-mates and he calmly walked back to the half-way line – still minus his shorts. No attempt was made to cover his bare backside until someone ran on with a fresh pair of shorts. Once the shorts were in Billy's hands his team-mates gathered round him to shield him from view whilst he pulled on the replacement shorts!

On the way home I asked my dad and big brother why all the players had gathered around him when he put his new shorts on. I was told that this was to protect his modesty. When I protested that everyone in the crowd had clearly seen his backside already – a cause of great amusement to the crowd in general and the ladies present in particular – they just laughed.

I was sold. From that day on whenever there was a clash of fixtures between Town and Fartown it was Fartown every time. Noticing my enthusiasm for this wonderful game my eldest brother, Len, gave me a book to read which had all the facts and figures about my home team. I read with interest how, in the period before the first world war, my team had dominated the sport. As I read about players like Rosenfeld, Wagstaff and Gronow, who were all record breakers, the more interested I became. I read about how my team had demolished a team in the cup by scoring over a hundred points with someone called Major Holland kicking a record number of goals. I pictured a man in soldier's uniform with a handlebar moustache kicking goal after goal.

Eventually I came across the section in the book about the Rorke's Drift test match, how the team, captained by Huddersfield's very own Harold Wagstaff, had won a famous victory against all the odds. I couldn't believe how ten men could possibly hold out against a full team of thirteen. It was a story that has stuck with me now for 60 years. For the last ten years or so I have been thinking about finding out more about the whole 1914 tour and writing a book about the Northern Union's most famous victory.

About a year and a half ago I finally decided to stop talking about writing a book and to actually have a go. I even started to draft an outline and structure. Then I built a research plan. I should point out at this stage that, before I retired, I was a Management Consultant specialising in project management, hence the detailed planning. Once I had identified what research I needed to do for the book I realised I had no idea where to start the actual research! I panicked and shelved the project.

But the writing bug had got me, so I set off to write a different book. Even as I was planning the Rorke's Drift book I had mentally worked out a structure for my second book. This book was all coming straight out of my head – no research needed. But would I be able to write sensible readable words and tell a story? Once I started, I couldn't stop. Writing the book – a semi-autobiographical novel about a bunch of sports mad kids growing up on a council estate who meet again many years later – was the easy bit. Getting a publisher was the real challenge. I soon learned that publishers were inundated with submissions from first time authors like myself. Eventually I turned to Amazon Kindle and self-published.

Next step? Back to my original goal – a book about the 1914 tour. With renewed confidence I went to my local library and started to scan the British Newspaper Archive. Gradually I acquired more and more information about the tour. I started reading about the development of Rugby league in Sydney and Auckland. Another critical individual came onto my radar – the remarkable Albert Baskerville. I had read snippets about the 'All Golds' but never realised the impact that this young postal clerk from Wellington, New Zealand, would have on the development of Rugby League as an international sport. The more research I did on the development of the sport in Australasia the more interesting it became. Instead of a chore the research turned into a hobby, I was having fun.

Sean Fagan's excellent book on the breakaway in Australia (The Rugby Rebellion) was invaluable as were the Australian and New Zealand newspaper archives. I went in search of information about Harold Wagstaff and his early life. I bought 'Best in the Northern Union', an account of the 1910 tour and 'Harold Wagstaff a Northern Union Man' (both good reads).

As an aside here – when the Wagstaff book came out I had a moment of panic as I thought someone had beaten me to the punch. I raced down to the Giants shop at the John Smith Stadium and bought it as soon as I could. On reading it I had a great sense of relief as I felt the scope of my book was quite different – I hope you will all agree.

The Rorke's Drift test was undoubtedly the pinnacle of this young man's career. But to follow it up by leading his Huddersfield team to glory on his return demonstrated to me the true greatness of the man. No resting on his laurels for this young man. Who knows what other achievements Wagstaff and his 'Team of All the Talents' might have achieved but for the intervention of the Great War.

From the very beginning I knew that I didn't want to write a factual account of what happened when and who scored what and where. As I have alluded to earlier this is a story that has fascinated me since my childhood and I wanted other people to share in the 'story'. My story is built on the facts, and real events underpin the story. To achieve that I have spent hundreds of enjoyable hours pouring over old newspaper articles, books and other publications. My aim in this book is to explore and develop the characters who made that time in the history of the game so special on both sides of the world.

I hope you will enjoy reading this book as much as I have enjoyed producing it. I expect that the Rugby League enthusiasts will be drawn initially to this book but I hope that after reading it you will pass it on to other people so that they can share in the beauty of the bravery of the Northern Union test team in that legendary third test at the SCG. After all, it is undoubtedly the greatest act of sporting bravery ever produced by a team representing the British Isles.

Finally my thanks go to Martyn Sadler and his team at League Express for their confidence in me and my book in what must have been a very difficult time for them. Thanks also to Dave Calverley at the Huddersfield Rugby League Heritage site for generously allowing me to use so many of the archive's pictures, including the image of Harold Wagstaff which apears on the front cover. To my new friends at the Rugby League Record Keepers Club and Rugby League Historians for their help and the individuals who generously responded to my request for pictures. Specifically, Neil Ormston, Andrew Hardcastle, Mike Baxter, Steve Fox, Steven Hibbert and Colin Booth many thanks for your help.

Finally, my thanks go to my wonderful wife, Susan, who has put up with me tapping away on her dining room table for all these hours with never a complaint. Without her support and encouragement, I would not be typing this now.

CHAPTER 1 – ONE GAME ALL WITH ONE TO PLAY

29th June 1914 – Sydney Cricket Ground

Harold Wagstaff, the captain of the defeated Northern Union side, was the last man to return to the dressing room. He had stayed on the field to shake hands and congratulate his opposite number on the Australian side, Sid Deane.

As he surveyed the scene in the dressing room, the disappointment amongst the exhausted players was evident. They had set out that day to secure the Ashes having convincingly beaten the home side by 23 points to 5 only two days earlier. Today, on Kings Day, a bank holiday in Australia, cheered on by 50,000 enthusiastic home fans, the Australian team had triumphed by 12 points to 7. The third and final test, therefore, would be the decider.

Wagstaff, a tall, fair haired centre three-quarter, went around the room and shook the hands of every single player. The last man he approached was his Huddersfield team-mate Douglas Clark, 'Well played Douglas' he said as he patted him on the back.

'Aye it wasn't to be today 'Arold.' Clark had disappointment written all over his face. 'Just our bloody luck losing Jack so early in the second half. Every time we lake here we finish wi' twelve men.'

'Aye and the bloody ref didn't help' another forward, Percy Coldrick, chimed in.

Douglas Clark continued 'I suppose we'll just have to make sure we finish the job in the third test.'

'Well we've got a few weeks to get some of the injured lads fit and back in the side before then' Wagstaff addressed the whole team. 'We've got the trip to New Zealand coming up, so we've got nigh on six weeks before the decider. We'll show them Aussies what Northern Union men are made of eh lads?' He clenched his right hand into a fist and drove it into his left hand it to emphasise the point.

A cheer went up from the rest of the team and there was a noticeable brightening of the mood in the dressing room.

At this point the joint managers of the touring party came in. The two men looked out of place in this environment, in their smart suits, white shirts with starched collars and official ties contrasting with the mud-spattered faces and kit of the players. The two managers were on their second tour of Australia, having been joint managers on the very first tour in 1910. On this tour the taller one, John Clifford, had been appointed as Team Manager and Joe Houghton was the General Manager.

Mr Clifford spoke first 'Well played lads, considering all the injuries we've had that was a very brave effort. Every one of you has played your heart out today. As you know we've got a busy week, with another match up at Bathurst on Thursday and then we've got a re-match with New South Wales on Saturday before we set sail for New

Zealand. Hopefully a few days at sea will give you all a chance to rest and refresh yourselves before we start the programme of matches over in New Zealand.'

At this point Mr Houghton took over 'We're expecting some tough matches over there lads. These New Zealand boys will be no mugs. They showed us that when we went there in 1910. Anyway gentlemen, there's a reception in town for us tonight so you can all let yourselves go a bit, you've certainly earned it. BUT remember you are all representing, not just the Northern Union but the whole of England[1]'.

'Don't forget us Welsh[2] boys Mr Houghton' chipped in Jack Chilcott.

'How could I forget you Welshmen Jack' replied Houghton. 'I stand corrected you are all representing the whole of Great Britain!' at which point another great cheer went up.

As the two managers left the changing room together they chatted. 'In all my time as a player and a manager' started Clifford 'I have never known a side get so many injuries. We were already down on numbers before the match but there's a few more lads in there who won't be fit to play for a couple of weeks at least'.

'Aye' Houghton replied 'this trip to New Zealand has come at just the right time for us. With a bit of luck, we could have some of them back, fit and ready to play.'

As the two men emerged from the building they were besieged by reporters.

'Why do you think your boys lost today Mr Clifford?' a reporter asked.

'Quite simple young man, the Northern Union lost to a better side today, credit where credit is due' Clifford replied diplomatically.

'What did you think of the crowd today, they're saying there were more than fifty thousand at the game?' asked another reporter.

'It really shows how popular the Northern Union game has become over here in your wonderful country' Houghton replied smugly. And well he might, the Northern Union had negotiated a deal with the New South Wales rugby authorities to receive 65% of all gate receipts at every game on the tour.

'Everybody over here is talking about your man Wagstaff, some say he's not as good as Dally Messenger' the quick-fire questions kept coming.

'I've seen Dally Messenger play a few times and he certainly is a talent' Clifford responded. 'It's a pity he retired before the series started it would have been good to see Harold up against him, maybe then the whole world could draw their own conclusions.' He paused for a moment, before adding 'Let me put it this way young man. If I had to choose between Wagstaff and Messenger I would pick Harold every time'.

'So, you're saying that Wagstaff is better than Messenger?' the reporter persisted.

'What I am saying is that in MY opinion Harold Wagstaff is the finest all-round player, captain and tactician I have ever had the pleasure to watch or manage. Is that clear enough? Now if you gentlemen will excuse us, we have some business to sort out.'

As the two men walked away a reporter shouted after them 'Is it true they're bringing the third test forward to next Saturday?'

The two men did not break stride or respond to this question but they certainly both heard it.

Later, as the two managers sat in the hotel bar, each

with a schooner of cold beer. Houghton leaned forward and spoke in hushed tones 'What did you make of that last question John?'

'D'you mean the one about the third test taking place on Saturday?' Clifford replied.

'Aye I do, I thought they'd agreed to wait till we come back from New Zealand. Has anyone told you about any changes?'

'Not a word Joe, not a word' Clifford paused and took a large swig of his beer. He wiped the froth from his moustache before continuing, 'But it wouldn't surprise me if the gentlemen running the New South Wales Rugby League did try to bring the game forward.'

'Well three test matches in eight days is a tall order for any team' reflected Houghton. 'And the Management Committee has already agreed to the match being delayed until after the New Zealand leg of the tour. Surely, they won't reverse the decision now. Especially when they know we have so many players injured.'

'Truth be told, I was a bit surprised when they agreed to put the test match back 'til after the New Zealand leg of the tour.' He paused for a moment and rubbed his chin as he assembled his thoughts. Eventually he leaned forward and spoke in hushed tones 'I reckon the New South Wales committee didn't expect their lads to level the series today. If we had won – and I think we would have done if Jack Robinson hadn't got crocked – the third test would have been a dead rubber[3], but now it's one test all....' he paused.

'There will be a lot of pressure on the league to play the game here in Sydney' Joe Houghton completed the sentence for his co-manager. 'Well if they do ask us to change it, what d'you reckon we should do John?' Houghton was looking worried.

'We will thank them politely for the request and then refuse it, that's what we'll do. Any way Joe, as of now, we don't have a request, do we? But we do have a match on Thursday up at Bathurst. So, tomorrow morning we'll check on the lads and see who's fit before we decide who to take with us to play. The rest of the lads can have a bit of time off and rest here in Sydney. God knows they've earned it.'

The two men finished their beers and arranged to meet in an hour's time in the hotel lobby for the short journey to the venue where the formal reception in their honour would take place. One player who didn't make it to the reception was the captain. Harold Wagstaff had received a bad knock to the head during the game and, although he carried on, the doctor later diagnosed a slight concussion and ordered him to bed for complete rest.

□□□

30th June 1914 Sydney

The following morning the players were gathered in the hotel lounge. Quite a few of them were showing signs of the hospitality they had enjoyed the night before. Others were limping and several were sporting cuts and bruises on their faces from the ferocity of the Australian tackling the previous day.

As they waited for the arrival of the managers the tour vice-captain, Willie Davies, was in deep conversation with his great friend and fellow Welshman Bert Jenkins. 'I tell you what Bert, you've got to give these Aussies their due they certainly know how to entertain a touring team, we were treated like royalty last night.'

'Aye we certainly were well looked after and, by the looks of it, some of the lads might have over done it. One or two are looking a bit worse for wear.'

'I'm just going to go round and check on who's fit to play up in Bathurst on Thursday. Mr Clifford and Mr Houghton will want to get the team sorted as soon as possible 'cos I've heard it's quite a long way up country.'

Davies took a small book out of his jacket pocket along with a pencil, which he carefully licked before writing on one side of the paper 'LADS FIT' and on the other side 'LADS NOT FIT'. He had a brief conversation with each of the players as he updated his list. When he had finished, he added up the lists.

As the two managers walked in Willie went up to meet them and they sat down at a table away from the other players and immediately went into a detailed discussion.

Meanwhile Gwyn Thomas who had played full back the day before asked Billy Jarman, the previous day's loose forward 'Have you put your name forward to play on Thursday Billy?'

'When Willie asked me if I was fit, I'd no option but to say yes. I'm not injured but I could really do with a rest. He said we were struggling to put a team out, so I reckon I'll be laking[4] on Thursday as well. How about you Gwyn, you took a knock didn't you?'

'Aye I reckon I need at least a week, there's no point making it worse is there?'

At that point John Clifford rose to his feet holding a piece of paper. He coughed to clear his throat and get everyone's attention. 'Now I would have liked to have given everybody who played yesterday a rest' he started 'but, as you all know lads, we have been hit very hard and have suffered a lot of injuries. So, the team who will travel with me up country to play the Western Districts at Bathurst will be as follows:

Full Back – I am pleased to say that Alf Wood has recovered from his injury and will play at Full Back.

Right Wing will be Frank Williams.' A ripple of applause followed each name that was announced along with words of encouragement.

'Right Centre is Billy Hall.

Left Centre is Willie Davies.

Left Wing will be Jack O'Garra.' O'Garra was normally a half back but the tourists were so short of fit wingers that he had been named on the wing.

'Stand Off Half is Stuart Prosser.

Scrum Half will be Johnny Rogers.

The front row will be 'Rattler' Roman, James Clampitt and Joe Guerin.

In the second row we have Jack Smales and Billy Jarman.

And, finally, 'Chick' Johnson will be at Loose Forward.

Jack Chilcott will accompany the side as the travelling reserve.' John Clifford carefully folded the piece of paper and put it in his jacket pocket. He continued 'I would particularly like to thank Frank Williams, the two Billy's and Johnny for making themselves available to play so soon after the test match. I would have liked to have given you all a few days' rest, but you all know the score as regards our injuries so, well done lads.'

As John Clifford sat down there was a round of applause and the lads who he had singled out and thanked all received congratulatory pats on the back and handshakes from their team-mates.

No sooner had John Clifford sat down than he stood up again, 'Oh and I forgot to mention the rest of the team will remain here in Sydney to enjoy a well-earned rest.' This particular announcement received the largest cheer of the day.

Joe Houghton stood up. 'I'd like to add my thanks to all of the lads who played in the test match and who have been selected for this next match. I've spoken to Harold this morning; he is much better, and he expects to be back on his feet tomorrow. So, for those of you who are not going up to Bathurst for the match on Thursday, he will be leading a light training session down at the sports field.'

This announcement did not enjoy quite the same reception as the previous one and there were a few moans from some of the players.

Douglas Clark was not pleased at this response and pointed out 'Don't forget lads we haven't achieved what we came here for yet. The run out on Thursday is to get rid of the stiffness from the last two games and gives us a chance to polish some of our skills and passing movements before the rematch with New South Wales. So, stop your moaning, we've got a job to do and I for one am determined we will do it.'

As the players made their way out of the hotel lounge Fred Longstaff approached his club mate Clark, 'Well said Douglas. Don't worry about the lads they'll be giving their all on Thursday whether they are up in Bathurst or down at the sports field. The lads will support you to the hilt.'

CHAPTER 2 – FROM FARMER'S FIELD TO FARTOWN

March 1906

'Run 'Arold run!'

Fourteen-year-old Harold Wagstaff was doing what he did best, breaking through the opposition defence and heading for the opposition line. As he made his way towards the try line, he heard a dog barking and saw an irate farmer sporting a long grey beard and waving a stick. The black and white sheep dog had his radar fixed on the young rugby player and was making a direct line for him. Quick as a flash Harold changed direction and headed away from the dog in the direction of Holmfirth. His friends had already set off and were 50 yards in front of him. As they piled over the dry-stone wall of the farmers field Harold caught up with them.

'That was a close call lads' gasped one of the rugby players, a burly dark-haired lad who was a good deal older than Harold, as they continued to jog along. By this time, the farmer had called the dog back but continued to shout angrily at the lads whilst waving his stick.

The group of young lads realised they were in the clear, so they relaxed the pace and started to walk down the hill into the centre of Holmfirth. 'I'm sick of being chased off in the middle of a match' replied Harold 'I'm gunna ask our Norman if I can lake for Underbank, on a proper pitch with proper markings and goal posts.'

'D'you reckon they'll let you play for 'em 'Arold? You're not old enough yet are yer?' a skinny ginger haired friend asked.

'Well Ginger me father always says when you're big enough you're old enough, I reckon I can hold my own with anyone.'

'Aye we were, weren't we lads? Until that bloody farmer chased us off, I was just about to score as well. D'you think they'd take me on at Underbank our Norman?'

'Well you might be in luck brother; I've done my leg in, so they'll be short of a centre. I tell you what I'll go with you to the next training session and introduce you if you like. But I can't guarantee you'll get a game y'know.'

'Oh, he'll be alright Norman he's already too good for us lot at the Pump Hole Rangers' Ginger offered re-assurance to Harold and his brother.

□□□

A few days later Harold was introduced to the coach at Underbank by his elder brother. 'This is my little brother, 'Arold. He's a bit raw Selwyn but he's a good laker and we're short of centres, what with me being injured and Freddy Beaumont joining up.'

Selwyn Lockwood eyed the new recruit up. 'Have you played much then young man?'

'Aye Mr Lockwood, I've been laking wi' Pump Hole Rangers for a while now. I think I'm ready to step up.'

Selwyn Lockwood put his right hand on Harold's shoulder 'Let's see how you go in training then lad, you can join in with that group over yonder laking touch and pass[5].'

As Harold followed his instructions and joined in enthusiastically Selwyn Lockwood turned to Norman, 'Well your brother doesn't look so little to me, how old is he then Norman?'

'He's just turned fifteen' came the reply 'but he can look after himself'. This was a lie as Harold was still a couple of months' short of his fifteenth birthday.

'He's a big lad for fifteen I'll give you that. It'll be interesting to see how he goes when we finish with a full-on game. I'll put him up against Johnny Blake and see how he handles that.'

'Bloody hell Selwyn, that's a bit harsh isn't it, putting him up against the biggest and dirtiest player in't team?'

'It's no different to what he'll face if I pick him for't first team on Saturday is it?'

'Aye right enough, I don't suppose it is.'

'Why don't you stick around and see how your 'little' brother gets on against the big lads Norman? You can help me out as well, we've a big turnout tonight so I could do with a hand.'

'Aye Selwyn, just tell me what you want me to do' replied Norman.

'Well I'm gunna split the forwards from the backs and I want to do some work with the forwards so you can get the backs working on some combinations while I do that.'

When Selwyn finished working with the forwards Norman sat down on one of the benches outside the club house and reflected on what might happen and what his father would say if Harold got injured by that monster Blake.

In the meantime, Selwyn Lockwood started to put the lads through their paces with some sprints, followed by a series of exercises. This, in turn, was followed by practicing some set moves.

Norman kept a watchful eye on his younger brother and was encouraged by the way Harold was able to more than hold his own with the physical challenges as well as the skills.

Eventually Selwyn blew his whistle and called the lads to gather round him. 'OK lads we'll finish off tonight in the usual way, we'll have a full contact game of rugby, ten minutes each way.' He then split the lads into two equal sides, taking care to ensure that Harold would be up against big Johnny Blake. Selwyn approached Blake 'The young lad' he pointed to Harold 'reckons he's ready to play with the big boys Johnny so see how he reacts to some hard – but fair – tackling.'

'OK Mr Lockwood you can rely on me.' Big Johnny Blake was relishing the task.

Norman could hardly dare to watch as the two teams lined up at the first scrum. Harold's team won the ball and it was quickly passed along the line to the young trialist. As he caught the ball Harold could see the huge figure of Johnny Blake bearing down on him. Quick as a flash he swayed to his right and then pushed off to the left. Blake made a despairing lunge at the young centre but – too late – he was gone. As the would-be tackler slid to the floor Harold was haring off towards the try line with only the full back to beat. As he approached the full back, he heard a team-mate yell 'inside', so he flicked the ball to his right where it was collected by a curly haired team-mate who took the pass and galloped his way to the try line.

Harold ran up to the try scorer to congratulate him and the two hugged each other in delight. Meanwhile, back on the half-way line a very angry Johnny Blake was being helped to his feet by one of his team-mates. 'What happened there Johnny, I thought you had him covered?'

'Aye so did I' Blake spat on the pitch as he replied. 'The slippery little bugger did me good and proper, but he won't be so lucky next time.'

Norman witnessed all this from his seat on the bench, well almost all of it. He had actually closed his eyes at the moment Johnny Blake went in for 'the kill', by the time he reopened them Harold was well on his way to setting up the try.

The next time Harold got the ball it was just in front of the club house and Norman had a clear view of Blake closing in on his brother, his face contorted in anger as he saw the opportunity for revenge. Harold saw him too and waited until Blake was committed to the tackle before slipping the ball out to his winger who sprinted over for a try. Blake didn't hold back and crashed into the younger Wagstaff. This late tackle so infuriated the older Wagstaff that he rushed onto the pitch and pulled Blake away from his brother.

'You dirty bugger' he shouted, 'that tackle was so late, are you trying to kill him or summat?'

The huge figure of Johnny Blake rose from the ground and towered over Harold's older brother 'Don't take it out on me, I'm just doing what I was told. Mr Lockwood told me to give him some stick to see what he's made of.'

By this time Harold had got back to his feet and walked over to Blake. He held out his right hand and said, 'Fine tackle sir' and the two players shook hands.

It was impossible to tell who was the most shocked, Johnny Blake or Harold's older brother, at this move by Harold. Just then Selwyn Lockwood arrived on the scene.

'What's going on here lads?'

Harold was the first to speak 'I was just complimenting Mr err err'

'Blake' replied an even more surprised Johnny Blake.

'I was just complimenting Mr Blake on a fine tackle' Harold explained.

'Aye and I was just complimenting young Mr Wagstaff here on a good pass' added Johnny Blake. The two players put their arms around each other in a congratulatory hug and from that moment the two were the very best of pals and Johnny Blake always looked out for young Harold.

Harold was duly selected to play the following Saturday against another local team from Milnsbridge and marked his debut with a brace of tries. Not surprisingly he was again selected the following week to play against the Huddersfield 'A' team, which was made up mainly of players who were professional, many of whom had turned out for the Huddersfield first team. Harold was excited at the prospect of testing his skills against these professionals and couldn't wait to tell his father and brother that he had retained his place in the team. However, when he told his father the good news, he received an unexpected response.

As he returned from training his father was sitting at the kitchen table, drawing on his pipe. 'Great news father[6], I'm in't team again this week, and guess what?'

'Well I'm not surprised lad, after scoring twice in your first game, they've got to pick you, 'aven't they.'

'Aye and we're playing Fartown's 'A' team, so it'll be a real challenge.'

'D'you mean the Huddersfield second team, but they're all professionals, aren't they?'

'Well most of 'em are, they might have a couple of triallists in the team though.'

'Now then lad, just sit the sen[7] down. I don't like the idea of you up against them professionals. You're not yet fifteen, yer bones are still developing.'

'Father I'm ten and a half stone, I can look after me'sen and don't forget Milnsbridge had some big fellas laking for them.'

'Aye lad I know, I was there. But their big lads were slow, and you were too fast and nippy for 'em. These professional lads will know every trick in the book and they'll soon sort a young whipper snapper like you out.' He paused before adding 'I don't think you should lake, you must tell Mr Lockwood that you're not available. And that's my last word.'

Harold could not hide his disappointment, but he knew that when his father made his mind up no amount of arguing from anyone would make him change it. He said good night to his father and quietly made his way to bed.

When Harold explained the situation to his brother the following day, Norman was sympathetic. 'What are you going to do then Harold?' he asked.

'I don't know Norman, I can't tell Mr Lockwood that me father won't let me play can I, he'll think I'm a right baby won't he.'

'Aye, right enough, it makes me look a bit silly as well 'cos I told him you were big enough and old enough to look after yer sen.'

'I'm just going to think on it for the time being and try to work out what's best. I don't want to go against me father, but I don't want to let the team down either.' The brothers then set off for their different workplaces. For once Harold, with a dark cloud hanging over him as he wrestled with his dilemma, was not his usual cheerful self.

Eventually Harold decided that his future rugby career was more important than complying with his father's instructions. After all, he reasoned, he hadn't *actually told* his father that he would not play.

When Saturday came around, he quietly gathered his kit together. All the while making sure that his father was out of the way before making his way to the ground. Underbank were not fancied to win the game against their professional opponents but it was a close affair. Eventually the professionals' extra experience enabled them to run out winners. A highlight of the game was a try by young Harold where he broke through the Huddersfield defence and ran three quarters of the length of the field to score.

His father was in the crowd that day and although he was annoyed that his youngest son had disobeyed him, he was brimming with pride when he saw Harold score that try. As Harold walked back to the halfway line after being congratulated by his team-mates, he caught a glimpse of his father on the side-lines and, to his great relief, he received an approving nod from him.

Unbeknown to Harold someone else in the crowd was taking note of the young centre's performance.

Joe Clifford was attending the match to monitor the performance of the two triallists in the Huddersfield side, but it was Underbank's try scoring centre who caught his eye.

Clifford was on the management committee of the Huddersfield team and, as he made his way to the dressing room, he made a point of shaking hands with Selwyn Lockwood, the Underbank trainer. 'Well played, your lads have put up a very brave show today Mr Lockwood, they've done you proud.'

'Thank you, Mr Clifford, we did our best, but your lot always had the edge on us' Lockwood replied.

'Who was that young fella who played in the centre for you?' Clifford asked.

'Oh, that's Norman Wagstaff's younger brother, it's only his second game for us. He's a bit raw but he has potential. He's nobbut[8] fifteen so he's plenty of time to improve.'

'Wagstaff you say, what's his Christian name?'

'I believe it's 'Arold, 'Arold Wagstaff.'

Joe Clifford pulled a small notebook from his pocket and scribbled down the name. 'Thank you, Mr Lockwood and very well played.'

That evening when Harold returned home, he was still buzzing with excitement from the game, but he did not know what to expect from his father. Harold knew he had gone against his father's wishes and he would have every right to reprimand him for that. On the other hand, there was that approving nod after his try. In the event nothing was said. He received neither scolding nor congratulations.

As he made his way to bed that night Harold was mightily relieved that his father seemed to have accepted that he was capable of playing open age football and he began to believe that his dream of playing professional rugby may, one day, come true.

As the season drew to a close Harold had become a regular member of the Underbank team. His brother Norman gave him great encouragement and went to watch every game in which his younger brother played.

As the two brothers walked home after the final game of the season Harold asked his brother 'D'you reckon your ankle will be OK next season Norman?'

'If only 'Arold, if only. The doctor says it'll be Christmas before I'm fit to start training and then I'll have to take it steady and build me muscles up again. It's a right pain in the arse not being able to lake, especially now my little brother is in the team. But I'm not as bad as some folk, Dick Jenkins did his knee a couple of years ago and the doctor says he'll never play again. Any road, I might not get back in't team now that young lad has settled into my place in't team'.

'How d'you mean Norman?'

'I mean you, you daft bugger. With all yer tries and goal kicks as well', Norman gave Harold a friendly push on the shoulder.

'Oh, gerraway Norman you'll be back, just think of it, the Wagstaff brothers in the centre for Underbank.'

'We'll see 'Arold, maybe one day.'

'Hey what about the New Zealand rugby team Norman, 'ave you been reading about them and the way they play?'

'Aye they're calling them the Invincibles aren't they.'

'Yes – cos nubdy can beat 'em. But have you heard about how they play though? They don't keep kicking the ball every time they get it. They pass the ball by hand and hold onto the ball; I've been thinking a lot about that. It doesn't make sense when you think about it. Why kick the ball and give it to the other side when you can keep it by passing to a teammate?'

'I reckon you 'ave a point there 'Arold' Norman scratched his head. 'I've noticed that you hardly ever kick the ball when you have it. Did you pick the idea up from reading about them Invincibles then?'

'Well them and Broughton Rangers[9], I've heard they play in a similar way and they're doing alright aren't they?'

'D'you know summat 'Arold?'

'What Norman?'

'I reckon I'll be able to get back in th'Underbank team when I get over my injury after all, 'cos you'll be off playing professional somewhere?'

'Well that's what I want to do actually' Harold had a slightly dreamy look on his face as his mind drifted off. 'Do you really think I could make it as a professional Norman?'

'I'd put me shirt on it 'Arold. With all your skills and then all that thinking you're bound to make it, mark my words. But don't go getting all big headed about it', he clipped his younger brother on the back of his head.

'Fancy all them New Zealanders coming halfway round the world just to lake football.' Harold's mind wandered again as he pictured himself on a boat, sailing to the other side of the world, wearing a blazer with the badge of the Northern Union on it.

'Wake up dreamer' Norman elbowed his brother 'it's cricket season now so just drop your kit off at home and let's go down to't cricket field and see how Holmfirth are doing. I'll see if I can sneak you a shandy without anyone noticing if you behave yourself' and the two brothers made their way down the hill from Underbank to Holmfirth, laughing and joking all the way to the cricket field.

November 1906

The 1906 – 7 season was a landmark season for the Northern Union. In an attempt to improve the game as a spectator sport the clubs had all agreed that the number of players be reduced from fifteen to thirteen a side. They also reduced the number of scrums by introducing the play the ball rule, whereby the tackled player was allowed to retain possession of the ball after being tackled, then get to his feet, place the ball on the floor and heel it back between his legs to a teammate. It was also the season when fifteen-year-old Harold Wagstaff would make his professional debut.

After playing a game for Underbank at Moldgreen Harold was approached by the match referee, George Dickinson.

'Now then young man' Dickinson began 'that was a good game, did you enjoy yourself?'

'Oh, I always enjoy a game of football sir; I look forward to Saturday all week and I can't wait to get on the pitch' came the reply.

'Aye, I it's quite obvious that you enjoy the game and I think you have a lot of talent.'

'Well thank you Mr Dickinson I really appreciate that' Harold shifted from foot to foot and blushed ever so slightly at this unexpected compliment.

'Well afore I took up refereeing I laked a bit with Halifax and I had a few games for Yorkshire as well. Have you ever considered playing for a professional team?'

'It's an ambition of mine actually, sir.'

George Dickinson moved a little closer to the young man and almost whispered 'I still have some contacts with the Halifax club, and I think they might be interested in signing a promising young player like yourself. How does that sound.'

Harold was taken aback by this unexpected approach and he stuttered 'Like I said Mr Dickinson I love playing football and I would like to play professional at some stage, and I'm not that bothered where I play.'

Unbeknown to the two of them the conversation between the young centre and the referee was observed by

Edgar Turner who was on the committee of the Underbank club. Turner was also a good friend of a certain Joe Clifford from the Huddersfield professional club and had been asked by Clifford to keep an eye on the development of the talented three-quarter.

After considering Harold's age the Halifax club decided not to follow up the suggestion of George Dickinson and sign the young man. However, just over a week later Harold and his father, Andrew, were sat reading the reports of the weekends sporting activities when there was a knock on the door. Harold got up and walked to the door where a gentleman in a suit and bowler hat was waiting.

'Hello, it's Harold isn't it?' The stranger took off his hat and held out his hand and a rather surprised Harold shook it. 'I'm Joe Clifford from the Huddersfield Cricket and Athletic Club and I would like to have a word with you on a matter of great importance. May I come in?'

'Who is it 'Arold?' the shout came from Harold's father.

Harold hesitated slightly before saying 'You'd better come in then Mr err Clifford.' He turned and led Mr Clifford into the kitchen. 'This is Mr Clifford from the Huddersfield club father.'

Andrew Wagstaff rose to his feet and shook hands with the visitor. 'And what can we do for you Mr Clifford' he said. As he spoke, he turned to his son 'Don't just stand there looking gormless 'Arold, get Mr Clifford a chair.'

Harold did as instructed, and the three of them sat down at the kitchen table.

Joe Clifford put his hand to his mouth and gave a cough to clear his throat and leaned forward as he addressed Andrew Wagstaff. 'It is regarding your son Harold. I have been monitoring his progress since I saw him play last year against our reserve side and I believe he has the potential to make a first-class rugby player.'

'You do know the lad's only fifteen, don't you?', came the abrupt reply.

'Yes, I am fully aware of Harold's age, but I have heard that other clubs have shown an interest in signing him and, as he is a local lad, I would like him to sign for his local team.'

Harold could barely hide his excitement 'What d'you think father?'

Andrew Wagstaff took a long drag on his pipe and slowly blew the smoke from his mouth, carefully directing it away from the table, as he pondered the proposition. He looked Harold in the eye and then addressed Joe Clifford 'I have to do what's best for the lad Mr Clifford' he paused, 'and I believe he needs another season in the junior league before signing for a professional team.'

Joe Clifford considered for a moment before replying 'I understand and respect your position Mr Wagstaff but let's not be too hasty. I will come back tomorrow when you have had chance to consider my proposal.' Joe Clifford rose to his feet 'And with that I will bid you good evening.'

Harold showed the visitor to the door. 'Thank you for coming Mr Clifford, it's like he says, father only wants what's best for me you know.'

'Yes, I appreciate that Harold. I will call again tomorrow about the same time.'

Harold closed the door and returned to the kitchen where his father was still sitting. 'You're too young 'Arold and that's an end to it.'

Harold knew that arguing with his father was a waste of time, so he settled back to reading the sports page of the local paper. At least he tried to read the sports news, but in reality, his mind was elsewhere as he dreamed of playing at Fartown for his local professional rugby team. The team his father had taken him as a young boy to watch many times.

The following morning Norman and Harold set off to walk to work in nearby Holmfirth. As they made their way down the hill Harold couldn't wait to tell Norman about the previous night's visitor.

'What did I tell you 'Arold, I said it was only a matter of time didn't I?'

'But d'you think father will change his mind and let me sign on? They're me local team and I've always supported them. It's me dream Norman. Will you have a word with father, he might listen to you?'

'In my experience 'Arold once father has set his mind there's no man on earth could get him to change it.'

Harold looked crestfallen.

Norman rustled his younger brother's hair with his right hand, 'Alright little brother, I'll have a word tonight. But I'm not sure if it will make any difference.'

'Oh, thanks Norman. Any road I'll si'thee[10] tonight then' and the two brothers separated and headed for their respective places of work.

Joe Clifford kept his promise and returned the following night only to receive the same answer. As he spoke to Andrew Wagstaff and listened to his negative response it was the expression on young Harold's face that he paid greatest attention to. There was just enough in the young man's controlled reaction to his father's negative response to encourage Joe Clifford.

Now, Joe Clifford was a determined and persuasive man and he did not give up on his quest to sign the young Harold Wagstaff. He had been impressed with the young lad the very first time he saw him play and the reports he had received since then only served to increase his interest. He continued his efforts to persuade Andrew Wagstaff to change his mind but further visits to the Wagstaff home on Wednesday and Thursday received the same response. As Harold Wagstaff made his way home from work on Friday evening, he had begun to accept that his professional rugby career would have to wait a while. However, when he entered the family home his father's greeting came as a complete – but pleasant – surprise. 'Now then lad you'd better put some decent clothes on we're going up to your uncle's place to meet yon Mr Clifford.'

Harold could barely fasten the buttons on his best shirt he was so excited. He was still tucking his shirt into his trousers as he rushed back downstairs and stumbled on the last two steps almost falling over.

'Calm down 'Arold, you don't want to go breaking your leg now do you?' his father joked.

'Sorry father I just didn't want to keep you waiting.'

'Oh, afraid of me changing my mind about meeting Mr Clifford, were you?'

'Course not father. But 'ave you changed your mind about me signing on for Huddersfield?'

'Well I got a message today from Mr Clifford saying he would like to meet again, and he had something special to say. And what with your brother and Mr Clifford nattering on at me and that hang dog look on your face I thought we might as well see what he has to say for himself.'

'But why are we going to Uncle Jack's place to meet him?' Andrew Wagstaff's brother was the licensee of the Druids Hotel in Holmfirth.

'That were his idea lad not mine.'

When they eventually arrived at the public house Joe Clifford was waiting to greet them. 'Good evening Mr Wagstaff.' They shook hands. 'Hello again Harold. Would you two like a drink?'

'I think I'll wait on it a bit thank you' Andrew Wagstaff replied. 'I'd like to hear what you've got to say wi' a clear head if you don't mind.'

'Very well. Gentlemen shall we take a seat', he pointed to a table by the window and the three of them sat down.

'Mr Wagstaff' Joe Clifford began 'I understand that you're concerned about your son's age and the danger of his young body getting damaged. I want to assure you that we will look after his welfare and make sure he develops to his full physical potential. What is more' he put his right hand into his jacket pocket. 'I have been authorised by the committee of the Huddersfield Cricket and Athletic Club to offer, as a signing on fee, five gold sovereigns[11].'

Joe Clifford spread the five coins out on the table, taking meticulous care to make sure they occupied as much space on the surface of the table as possible.

Andrew Wagstaff looked long and hard at his youngest son. He saw a tall, strong young man and he saw in the expression on his face just how much this would mean to his son. He also studied Joe Clifford and could see a man of integrity. Determined, yes but as Andrew Wagstaff looked into his eyes, he saw an honest man, a man who would keep his word and would take care of his son.

Eventually, after what seemed to Harold like an age, he spoke in typical Yorkshire fashion 'Well, I can see that you will never leave us in peace until we agree, and I know my lad is keen. So, the answer is yes, but I don't want you messing the lad about. He's a good honest lad and he's a hard worker.'

'Thank you, Mr Wagstaff, you will not regret your decision.' Joe Clifford then turned and addressed Harold 'Your father has given his consent Harold; will you be happy to sign for the Huddersfield Club?'

'Aye I will indeed Mr Clifford, but I have just one condition.'

'And what's that lad?'

Harold took a deep breath, 'I'd like to get a game with the first team as soon as possible.'

Joe Clifford smiled 'The team for this week has already been picked but we have a match against Bramley a week tomorrow. We'll see how you go in training next week and if Mr Bennett, our trainer, is happy with you then you shall play.'

Joe Clifford pulled a document out of his pocket along with a pen and the three sat down and signed the form.

'Harold, I am pleased to say that you are now a player for the Huddersfield Cricket and Athletic Club. Now then Mr Wagstaff, what about that drink?' and they all shook hands. Fifteen minutes later Joe Clifford could be seen leaving the Druid's Hotel clutching the signed form and wearing a broad smile on his face.

An early picture of Harold Wagstaff (back row 2nd from left) in his Pump Hole Rangers days. (Courtesy Steven Hibbert)

CHAPTER 3 – MEANWHILE IN NEW ZEALAND THINGS WERE STIRRING

1906 Wellington, New Zealand

It was a quiet day in the Wellington Central Post Office and the two clerks were passing the time discussing the fortunes of their local rugby union team.

'I heard that a selector for the Wellington Regional team was at the match on Saturday and it seems he was very impressed by your performance, Bert' said a tall and gangly blond-haired man in his early twenties.

'D'you reckon Dick?'

'Sure do Bert, my mother was at the game and she was talking to the club chairman after the match. He said you were one of the three players who the selector named that had impressed him.'

'Yeh? Well I won't hold my breath on that one Dick. I had good form all last season, but they didn't pick me then, why would they now?'

'Well the team's announced next week so you'll find out

soon enough.'

At that point a tall, well-built man strode though the door of the Post Office and made his way up to the counter. 'I need to send this parcel back home[12], could you tell me how much it's going to cost please?'

Albert Baskerville pushed his colleague aside so that he could serve the customer. 'Good morning sir, just pass me the parcel and I'll weigh it, and it's to go to England is that correct?'

'Yeh that's right' came the reply.

'Say aren't you Billy Wallace the All Black centre?' Albert asked.

'That's right for my sins' he looked slightly embarrassed and smiled.

'Weren't you on the tour to the old country? You were the top scorer if I remember rightly.'

'Well, you're right on both counts Mr err?'

'Baskerville err Albert Baskerville at your service' Albert held his hand out and they shook hands.

'That name sounds familiar, are you a footballer too?' Billy Wallace enquired.

Albert's face beamed with pleasure that someone as famous as Billy Wallace recognised his name. 'Yes, I play for Oriental, the same team as Fred Roberts.'

'Really? I toured with Fred back in 1905.'

'Mr Wallace, could I ask a favour of you?'

'Ask away young man, it depends what you want. Any friend of Fred's is a friend of mine?'

Albert checked his watch – 12.55 – the office would be closing for lunch in about five minutes. He looked appealingly at his colleague, Dick, who had been observing the conversation with interest.

'Go on Bert you get off I can hold the fort for five

minutes; we're hardly run off our feet are we.'

'Oh, cheers mate'. He turned his attention to Billy Wallace 'Can I buy you lunch Mr Wallace? That's if you can spare half an hour?'

Billy Wallace checked his watch and did a quick calculation 'OK Albert but you've only got thirty minutes as I've got a train to catch at two o'clock'.

Albert guided his famous customer to a nearby café where they ordered two sandwiches and cups of tea.

'OK Albert you have my undivided attention, how can I help?'

Albert cut to the chase 'I'm writing a book about rugby Mr Wallace and I would like to know about your experiences on the tour back home, you must have had a whale of a time.'

'OK, Albert here goes. And cut the Mr stuff it's Billy to my friends. The tour was great. To travel over to the old country and play matches in England, Scotland, Ireland and Wales was really something special. We even played a couple of games in North America and one in Paris. It was the trip of a lifetime and we met lots of great people'. He paused 'But it wasn't all positive.'

'What parts didn't you like Mr err Billy?'

'Well the weather for one thing. I didn't realise how cold it was over there in the winter. Leeds in the middle of December was seriously cold'. He gave an unintentional shiver as his mind went back to 13th December 1905 in Leeds when the New Zealanders beat a Yorkshire select side by 40 points to nil.

Albert was scribbling all this down and he had barely touched his sandwich as he encouraged Billy to tell him more. 'You said that the weather was one of the things you didn't like about the tour, were there other negative things?'

'Did you read in the newspapers, Albert, about the financial success of the tour?'

'Yes, I did, it was a gamble wasn't it, but it certainly paid off. If I remember rightly it was very profitable.'

'Yes, that's all true, but we – the players that is – didn't get to share in the success. We were just on a flat three bob a day expenses. Whereas the managers, they had a great time being entertained and treat like royalty and all the while we were struggling to feed ourselves.'

'Wasn't that to do with your amateur status though? If you'd been paid you would have been regarded as professionals, wouldn't you?'

'Yeh that's what the big wigs said, but we weren't happy. Did you know that some of the clubs in England have broken away from the Rugby Football Union just so they can pay their players expenses?'

'Yeh I think I read a bit about them – are they the ones they call the Northern Union?'

'You're right again Albert. In fact, some of the lads on tour were approached to sign for the professional clubs over there, and I wouldn't be surprised if some of them don't take up the offer and move over there.'

'You didn't get to play against this Northern Union lot, though did you? I heard most of their best rugby players had switched over to them.'

'Yeh, we never got to play them so some of the wins – like the 40 nil against Yorkshire – were a bit hollow.' He leaned forward and in a low voice added 'Did you know the Managers were offered a load of dosh to play against a Northern Union select side?'

Albert was taken aback 'Really? What happened Billy?'

'Ah the Managers turned them down. The players would

have loved to have a go against the pros. Anyway, Albert that's enough of the negatives, tell me about this book of yours.'

'Well Billy, I have been studying the way we play the game in New Zealand so the book will be called "*Modern Rugby Football: New Zealand Methods; Points for the Beginner, the Player, the Spectator*". In fact, the tour by your lot – the Invincibles – was the inspiration for the book. I followed it avidly in the newspapers. It's just a shame you lost that one game against Wales[13] otherwise you would have had a perfect record'.

'Yeh sure, but we didn't play so well that day and fair play to Wales they came with a plan and executed it to perfection. Mind you Albert, Bob Deans will swear on his deathbed that he scored a try, but the referee said he was short of the line.' Billy Wallace checked his watch. 'Thanks for the lunch Albert and good luck with the book, I'm afraid I've got to dash.'

The two men stood up and shook hands 'Thanks a lot for your time Billy, it was a real pleasure meeting you.'

Albert sat down again and took a bite of his almost untouched sandwich. As he slowly chewed it the germ of an idea flashed into his head. He put down his sandwich, picked up his pen and scribbled the words *Northern Union* followed by a huge question mark.

CHAPTER 4 –
WHILST ACROSS
THE TASMAN SEA
IN AUSTRALIA

1905 Sydney, Australia

The Northern Rugby Union had been formed in 1895 when twenty-two of the north's top rugby clubs broke away from the control of the Rugby Football Union, primarily over the matter of paying players for 'broken time'. Up until this time Rugby Union had been a totally amateur sport played mainly by the privileged and professional classes. The sport was run by the Rugby Football Union and payment of any kind to players was deemed to be totally unacceptable.

The Northern Clubs argued that many of their players were working class and, as such, could not afford to take time off work to play rugby. The payment, therefore, for broken time was a way of compensating their players for loss of earnings. Despite the protests of the Northern Clubs the ruling body would not budge, so reluctantly the Northern Clubs decided, at an historic meeting at the George Hotel in Huddersfield, to set up their own union which would be called the Northern Rugby Football Union.

Ten years later, whilst the young Harold Wagstaff was starting out in senior football with his local team, Underbank, the seeds of a similar movement towards professionalism were starting to take root in New South Wales and New Zealand.

Around the same time a young man, who was to become the darling of Australian rugby and a key figure in the breakaway, was starting to attract increasing numbers of spectators to the sport.

As a child Herbert Henry Messenger developed a pot belly that was reminiscent of the one that the Attorney General of New South Wales, William Bede Dalley had. This led to the young boy being nicknamed after the illustrious politician. In this young man's case the nickname stuck with him throughout his life, although the 'e' was lost somewhere along the way.

Like his English contemporary, Harold Wagstaff, Dally Messenger's potential was spotted by senior clubs whilst he was playing junior rugby, in his case with the Warrigals club in Sydney. Unlike Wagstaff, however, Messenger was in no hurry to step up to the senior grade. In fact, he rejected a number of requests before agreeing to join the Eastern Suburbs club in 1905 at the age of twenty-two. In his first season with the Eastern Suburbs reserve side he was the star performer as they won the Second-Grade final beating the much fancied Glebe II side in a play-off.

His talent was clear, but his unorthodox style did not, initially, endear him to all of the selectors. After a particularly good performance from Dally in a second team game he was approached by one of the selectors. 'Well played young man.'

'Thank you, Mr Jameson.'

'That was an incredible piece of ball skills you showed to score your third try, where did you learn to do that?'

'Oh that, nobody taught me how to do it' Dally looked slightly embarrassed. 'I just go with my instincts. I saw their defence pushing up, so I just put the ball in the air and followed it up. Luckily for me it worked out.'

'Well Dally I'm going to put your name forward for the first grade when we meet to select the team for next week.'

'Thank you Mr Jameson I'm just happy to be playing footy, it doesn't bother me which team I'm in.'

When the selectors met on the following Tuesday evening Bob Jameson duly kept his word and proposed that Dally Messenger be selected to play stand-off half for the first grade. His suggestion wasn't universally accepted and met some opposition, notably from the first grade coach, Dick Regan. 'I'm not sure about selecting him for the first grade just yet. Yes, he's got talent, but I'm not convinced he will fit in with the systems we play. He's so unpredictable, no-one knows what he's going to do next. In fact, I don't think he even knows himself.'

'Come on Dick that's the very reason we should be picking him isn't it, his unpredictability?'

'Yeh, I've seen him do some brilliant stuff and he does stand out in the reserve grade. I don't think he'll get away with some of his tricks when he steps up to the higher standard of first grade. The experienced blokes we play against will soon work him out.'

'Well I vote we give him a try next week, all those in favour?'

Enough hands went up for the young man to be selected.

The season was drawing to a close, so Dally Messenger played just two games for the first grade that season. He must have done enough to win over the doubters as he became a regular selection in the following season. The spectators loved his style of play and attendances increased as word got around about his wizardry with the ball.

After a particularly mesmerising performance Bob Jameson and Dick Regan were sat in the club bar discussing the game. 'Well Dally did the business again today Dick. Aren't you glad you took my advice and promoted him to the first grade? Our supporters absolutely love him.'

Dick Regan took a big slug of beer before replying 'Yeh, I've got to admit you were certainly right Bob That's about the fourth time this season he has turned the game in our favour with his ball skills and his little tricks, not to mention his kicking which is immaculate. But you know, he's a difficult player to coach.'

Bob Jameson almost choked on his beer 'Oh come on Dick you can't be serious; the lad's just won the game for us almost single handed and you're complaining.'

'OK, OK Bob. Let me give you an example. Thursday night's training session we're working on some drills, practicing some set moves from the line out. Dally's second receiver, so he's supposed to draw his opposite number in and then release it to his centre. We run through it a couple of times and it works like clockwork. So, the first line out we get the captain calls the move. The lads all know what they are supposed to do. So, Dally gets the ball, draws his man in, but instead of releasing the ball to the centre he spins around and heads off in the opposite direction. It's so frustrating for me and the other players.'

'Are you referring to that time when he beat three or four men and got the ball out to Jim on the wing, who touched down in the corner?'

'Yeh, you're right and I shouldn't complain, but that's what's so frustrating. He's having a great run at the moment and getting away with it because it's so unexpected but once the other teams figure him out, he could become a liability.'

'You're a hard man to please Dick Regan. The guy makes a try and you're unhappy 'cos he didn't follow the plan. I give up.' Bob Jameson threw his hands in the air and shook his head in disbelief. 'Anyway, I understand the New South Wales selectors have heard about Messenger's talents and they are lining him up to be selected at centre, maybe that's a better position for him to unleash his trickery.'

'That's an interesting thought Bob. We'll have to wait and see how he goes at centre then.' Dick Regan looked thoughtful as he emptied his schooner and turned to his friend 'My shout Bob, same again?'

CHAPTER 5 –
BASKERVILLE'S
NEW PROJECT

1907 Wellington, New Zealand

The morning rush at the Wellington Post Office had died down and Dick Callam and Albert Baskerville were enjoying a well-earned cup of coffee. Albert reached into his leather satchel and, with an extravagant gesture, pulled out an envelope.

'What've you got there Bert?' Dick enquired.

Albert had a very self-satisfied look on his face 'This, my good friend is a letter from my publishers, the renowned company Gordon & Gotch.'

'Have they accepted your book then Bert?'

'Aye Dick they most certainly have.'

'Is that why you're speaking so posh, gone up in the word have you? Would you like me to refer to you as Mr Baskerville from now on then?'

Albert continued the pretence 'Yes my man, Mr Baskerville will be fine henceforth.' The two friends exchanged glances and then Albert's face finally slipped and they both burst out laughing. Their revelry was interrupted by a customer who approached the counter.

After a split second of panic the two of them recognised

John Dixon, a team-mate of Albert's from the Oriental rugby club. 'And what's causing all the frivolity this morning then?' he asked.

'Oh, take no notice John it's Bert he's got a publisher for his book, reckons he's going up in the world he does.'

'Congratulations Bert, when will the masterpiece be unleashed on the general public?' John Dixon held out his hand and Albert leaned across the counter to shake it.

'A couple of months I think, all being well.'

'Very good. Now is there any chance that the distinguished author could come down off his lofty perch and weigh this small parcel for me?'

Dick Callam was creased with laughter. 'I suppose I'd better do it' Albert gave his colleague a black look. 'As you can see my colleague here is indisposed at present' which only made Dick laugh even more.

The parcel was duly dealt with and John Dixon made his way out of the Post Office.

'Pull yourself together Dick, it's a good job that was a mate who came in and not an important customer, you could have got us in serious bother.'

When Dick finally regained his composure, he asked 'Will you be leaving your job here then Bert?'

'Don't be daft, you don't get rid of me so easily' replied Albert. 'Now the book's finished though I'm going to be putting a lot of energy into my latest project.'

'What sort of a project have you got in mind Bert?'

'Well it's very early days yet, Dick, but' he paused for a moment. 'D'you remember when Billy Wallace came in here a few months ago?'

'D'you mean the time when you sloped off early for lunch and left me running the shop?' the statement was loaded with sarcasm.

'There's no need to say it like that Dick, you said it was OK. And yes, that was the occasion I was referring to.'

'Sorry Bert, go on what's your meeting with Billy Wallace got to do with your new project?'

'Well I was asking him about the All Black's tour of the old country in 1905 when I got this idea. He said that the tour had been a great financial success, but the poor players didn't get to share in the profits. He also said that they didn't get chance to play all the best teams because the northern clubs had broken away and formed their own Union so they could pay their players for broken time'.

'What d'you mean by broken time?'

'It's paying the lads for wages they lost by playing rugby instead of working. Anyway, it kind of got me thinking about setting up a tour but this time playing all the top northern clubs and sharing the proceeds out amongst the players.'

'But won't that make all the players professionals Bert?'

'Not if we do it in a clever way. Look have you heard of Victor Trumper?'

'The cricketer from Australia?'

'Yeh, that's the one.'

'What about him?'

'Well he organised a very successful cricket tour to the Old Country. The players all had to pay to go on the tour and then they shared out the profits. The cricketers didn't get paid for playing they just got what you might call a 'return on their investment' so they're still classed as amateurs.'

Dick looked doubtful 'How many players do you think will want to go on the tour and risk their amateur status though?'

More than you might imagine' Albert took a furtive look around to check that no one was listening. 'Dick, this is all top secret. Not a word to a soul, if this gets out my project could be scuppered. I've also made contact with some very influential people in New South Wales who are extremely interested in us taking a team over there for a couple of games on the way to the Old Country. There are moves going on across the water to set up a professional league like the one they have in England.'

'All this intrigue is really exciting, do you need somebody to carry your bag Bert, I'm available?'

'I'm not joking Dick; this is serious stuff. I've even written to the Secretary of the Northern Union to see if they would be interested in such a tour.'

'And what did they say then?'

'Well I haven't heard yet but I'm expecting a reply any day now actually. I'll tell you once I get the response from them.'

Exactly one week later Albert Baskerville was terminating his employment at the Wellington Post Office. As he walked back to the counter after seeing his manager, he couldn't wait to tell his good friend the news. 'It's on Dick, the tour is on' Albert waved a piece of paper at his friend. 'I received this very enthusiastic cablegram from the Northern Union this morning and they are all for it. I've handed in my notice this morning so that I can concentrate on making all the arrangements for the tour.'

'But what will you live off Bert if you haven't got a salary from the Post Office?' Dick's concern for his friend was genuine.

'I've spoken to my publishers and they are arranging to bring the publication of my book forward and they've even offered to pay me an advance if I need it.' He paused for a moment 'And I've got enough put by to see me through until the tour starts.'

'Was the invite from the Northern Union unconditional then?'

'Pretty much Dick, they just need an assurance that I can get a strong team together for the tour and I've already got enough acceptances from some of our top players to cover that. It's going to be a bit tight time wise though, as I've only got just over four months to set it all up.'

'My god Bert you don't half make life difficult for yourself don't you.'

'You could say that Dick, but I'm confident I can pull it off.'

'What's the next step then Bert?'

'The first thing I need to do is to communicate with my contacts in Australia. One is a businessman called Giltinan and the other is Victor Trumper. They're based in Sydney, so I'll give them the good news about the tour being on. The last time I was in touch with them they said a visit from a team of New Zealand tourists could be the tipping point for professionalism over there.'

'Are you talking about Victor Trumper, the cricketer? The bloke you said organised a professional cricket tour of the Old Country, the one where they shared out the profits?'

'The very same Dick.'

'But who's the other fella, Guiltyman, what's he got to do with it?'

Albert stifled a laugh at his friends mistake, 'James Giltinan is the name and he's the money man. He's a top businessman and he's going to fund the launch of the professional league over in Sydney. What's more Dick...'

Their conversation was abruptly interrupted by a man

and his wife who were making a noisy entrance to the post office. The man was obviously in his wife's bad books as she proceeded to chastise him for his forgetfulness. She marched up to the counter and addressed Dick Callum 'Now then young man, how long does it take for a letter to reach England?'

'That'll take about six weeks madam' Dick replied with a smile.

The woman did a quick calculation. 'But that's too long. My niece will be married in just over four weeks' time. My stupid husband here was supposed to post this greetings card three weeks ago and I have just found it in his jacket'. She waved a rather dog-eared envelope in the general direction of her husband. 'You stupid man, I knew I shouldn't have given you the responsibility of a simple job like posting a card!' For a moment it looked like she was going to hit him with the card but at the last minute she swapped the card into her left hand and replaced it with her parasol with which she struck him a heavy blow to the head. He staggered back from the force of the blow before turning away and making for the door followed by his angry wife who continued hitting him on the back with the parasol.

The two clerks looked at each other in disbelief and then burst out laughing.

'Poor bugger' sighed Albert 'I don't know about you Dick, but I think I'll stay single.'

'Never mind all that nonsense Bert. You were just about to spill the beans about your Mr Giltinan before they came in.'

'Oh yes. Do you know who the most popular footy player in the whole of Australia is, Dick?'

Herbert Henry (Dally) Messenger had the distinction of representing both Australia and New Zealand in international matches.

'Well that's got to be Messenger hasn't it?'
Albert raised his eyebrows but kept his mouth firmly closed.

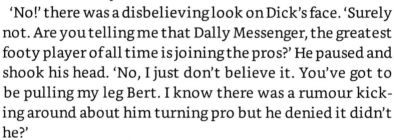

'No!' there was a disbelieving look on Dick's face. 'Surely not. Are you telling me that Dally Messenger, the greatest footy player of all time is joining the pros?' He paused and shook his head. 'No, I just don't believe it. You've got to be pulling my leg Bert. I know there was a rumour kicking around about him turning pro but he denied it didn't he?'

'I'm saying nothing Dick, but watch this space.' The reply was followed by a feint nod of the head. Albert leaned towards his friend and whispered 'Not a word, Dick. Not a single word.'

CHAPTER 6 –
THE BIRTH OF
PROFESSIONALISM
IN THE COLONIES

13th August 1907 – Sydney

Despite the opposition of the New South Wales and New Zealand Rugby Football Unions the team of New Zealand All Blacks, assembled by Albert Baskerville, duly arrived in Sydney. Arrangements had been made for them to play a series of three games against a New South Wales team which had been selected from the players who had already signed contracts to play in the New South Wales Professional Rugby League. The organisers were the aforementioned James Giltinan and Victor Trumper along with a famous politician named Henry Hoyle who had been elected president of the new league. The games would be played under rugby union rules as neither team had yet witnessed a game played under Northern Union rules.

The tourists timing was perfect. The formation of the New South Wales Rugby League had been confirmed only five days earlier at an historic meeting at Bateman's Hotel in Sydney.

The new sport had many doubters in the press as well as a lot of outright opposition. The Sydney Herald had even christened the touring team as the All Golds rather than the All Blacks. A name which had nothing to do with the colours worn by the team but rather as a dig at the players who – for the first time – would be able to share in any profits generated by the matches they took part in.

The man in the street, however, had a different perspective. The mainly working-class population of Sydney had no bias against professionalism and consequently interest in the series of matches was extremely high. There was an excited buzz in Sydney in the run up to the first match which would take place on the

The New South Wales squad which played against Albert Baskerville's New Zealand team.

17th August at the Royal Agricultural Showground. The presence of the fans favourite, Dally Messenger, in the NSW side added greatly to the anticipation.

It was a gamble and the man who had most to lose was James Giltinan. It was Giltinan and his co-conspirators, Victor Trumper and Herbert Hoyle, who had the vision to set up the first ever professional league in Australasia. The opportunity to play the touring NZ team was too good to miss. Giltinan saw this as the ideal way of generating interest amongst the sporting public of New South Wales and launching the new sport.

Albert Baskerville had also recognised the importance of the games and he had managed to negotiate a guarantee of £500 for his team to play a three-match series in Sydney.

When the touring party arrived in Sydney after a difficult passage from New Zealand, James Giltinan was standing on the dock waiting to welcome Albert Baskerville and his team.

As Albert Baskerville walked down the gangplank, he was amazed at the size of the crowd which had assembled to welcome them. He felt a surge of pride as James Giltinan held out his hand which Albert shook energetically.

'Welcome to New South Wales Albert' he declared.

'Thank you, Mr Giltinan, and what a pleasure it is to be here and to receive such a warm welcome' came Albert's reply. 'I never dreamed we would be celebrated in such an enthusiastic way.'

'These are exciting times Albert, the sporting world is shifting here in New South Wales and across the whole of Australia. The public has a real appetite for sporting entertainment, and I firmly believe the sport of Rugby League is going to become the premier sport in our young nations. In years to come you, and your All Black team-mates, will be recognised as being in the vanguard of this great movement.'

Albert was taken aback by the accolade placed on his initiative. He was well aware that his All Blacks were breaking new ground but until that moment he had not realised the true impact that they were about to make. Eventually he composed himself and responded. 'That is most generous of you Mr Giltinan, I hope that we will give a good account of ourselves in the forthcoming series and that the sporting public of New South Wales are not disappointed.'

'I am sure that that will not be the case Albert, and please drop the formality and call me James.' He leaned forward and spoke quietly to ensure he was not overheard 'We must speak privately later as I have news about the proposition which I mentioned to you in our earlier correspondence and which I believe will work out to our mutual benefit.' He gave a slight nod of his head with the merest hint of a wink. 'Perhaps we can speak at dinner tonight, a reception has been arranged for you and your colleagues at a hotel in town and my business partners, Victor Trumper and Herbert Hoyle, will be there and I know that they are very much looking forward to making your acquaintance and meeting the rest of your touring party'.

'I'm sure that the team will be delighted to attend the dinner James' replied Albert. 'And I'm very much looking forward to meeting your colleagues.'

'Now tell me Albert how was the voyage, I hear the weather has not been too kind.'

'You are correct James, the trip was dreadful, and consequently a number of the team are a little worse for wear, but I'm sure they will recover now that we have reached dry land. Though I fear that a few of them will not be well enough to attend tonight's reception.'

The two continued to exchange small talk as they waited for the touring party's luggage and kit to be unloaded from the vessel. When everything had been landed safely, they shook hands and agreed to talk further at dinner that evening.

Horse drawn carriages had been provided to transport the team to their hotel. The players appreciated the welcome and special treatment which had been laid on for them and happily acknowledged the cheers and waves from the residents of Sydney as they made their way in some style through the bustling city.

Albert's earlier analysis of the state of the team proved accurate and several players declined to join the group for the reception, preferring to take the opportunity to rest up on dry land after their unpleasant experience on the boat crossing.

George Smith, himself an original All Black tourist, had been involved in setting up contact with the Australians and had been appointed vice-captain of the touring team. As they arrived at the hotel, Albert pulled him to one side. 'I would like you to sit with me at dinner tonight so that I can introduce you to the people who are organising the professional game over here, George. I know that you've been involved in negotiations with Mr Giltinan and he's indicated that he has a proposition for us which will work to our advantage and I would like you to be there alongside me.'

'It would be an honour Bert, but do you know what this 'proposition' will entail?'

'I have a good idea that it might involve one of the New South Wales players joining the touring party for the trip back to the Old Country.' Albert tapped his nose with his right forefinger in a conspiratorial manner. 'And I don't just mean any player George. I think it will be one of their star players. But not a word of this to the other lads, it will just be between the two of us for the time being. I believe that Mr Giltinan will want to make a formal announcement to the press in due course and we don't want the story to leak out.'

'You can rely on me Bert, I won't say a word'. And with

that the two of them made their way to their hotel rooms to freshen up in preparation for the evening's entertainment. A certain George Smith was racking his brain to work out who this mysterious candidate from the New South Wales team could be.

When they arrived at the reception that evening there was a welcoming committee waiting for them comprising Giltinan, Trumper and Hoyle. Albert strode to the front and heartily shook hands with the three hosts and then proceeded to introduce the players individually to the trio.

As they eventually made their way to the dinner tables James Giltinan steered Albert and George to the top table. When they finally took their seats, he spoke to them both 'As you will have noticed we have several gentlemen of the press in attendance tonight. As I'm sure you will appreciate this is a major event in Sydney and the interest amongst the general public here is extremely high, so our every move is being scrutinised. Now as soon as everyone is seated Victor here, will say a few words of welcome and raise a toast to you and your team, but the main speeches will come after dinner has been completed. I will make the first speech and then you will be invited to respond, is that alright?'

'Yes, James that's perfectly fine. I have a short speech prepared for just such an occasion, but tell me are you intending to announce the inclusion of the star player in our touring party at this juncture?'

'No, I think we will leave that until after the three matches have been played. But don't worry the lad has signed up. Can you believe that he told me he was happy to take part, but I had to get his mother's permission first.'

'Really?'

'Yes, indeed Albert and, I'll tell you what, she drove a very hard bargain too. Quite a negotiator Mrs Messenger turned out to be. I'll go through the fine details with you tomorrow. Now that's enough of the business let's enjoy our meal.'

The press had gathered outside the hotel where the reception was taking place and did their best to extract any information from the guests as they arrived for the dinner. That they were unsuccessful owed much to the fact that most of the players probably knew less than the press and the ones who were in the know – Albert and the Australian trio – had already agreed to remain tight lipped and not disclose any information at this time. James Giltinan had agreed that the reporters would be admitted in to hear the speeches which followed the dinner and that he and Albert would do a brief question and answer session in the hotel foyer after the formalities had been completed.

As Albert and James Giltinan made their way to the foyer of the hotel for the Q & A session James gave Albert a short coaching session on how to handle the local press. 'The press here in Sydney are hungry for information Albert, the whole issue of professionalism is the number one topic at the moment. Our job here, tonight, is to give them just enough information to provide them with material for tomorrow's edition; but not to give the whole game away. We want them to see us as their friends as we want them to present the new league in a positive light, but we also need to keep them guessing a little bit so that we can feed them more titbits tomorrow and keep our story on the front pages of the papers.'

'I never realised that the papers could be managed in

such a way James. My natural inclination would be to tell them everything, but I can see the value in feeding them a bit at a time. It makes complete sense to me now that you have explained it.'

As the questions came in from the assembled mass of reporters Albert listened and learned from a master. He observed with interest the way that James Giltinan was able to handle the questions giving just enough information to satisfy their appetite without revealing everything. Eventually the reporters' attention turned to Albert.

'And how do you justify the fact that you have made these players lose their amateur status Mr Baskerville?'

'In the first place I would point out that the players on this tour are not professionals. They are not being paid to play rugby football. Each and every one of them has made a financial investment in the tour and if – and I must emphasise only if – the tour is a financial success and turns over a profit the players will take a share of those profits based on the size of their investment. I believe that that is a fair and equitable way of remunerating them for the financial risk they are taking.'

'What about the strength of the team you are bringing here to New South Wales, does it represent the best footballers from New Zealand?'

'The short answer to that is yes. We have brought over some of the finest players New Zealand has ever produced; and I am confident that the players who make up this touring party will give a good showing not only in the forthcoming games against the pride of New South Wales, but also when we meet the cream of the Northern Union when we reach the Old Country.'

'And what do you make of the New South Wales squad of

players Mr Baskerville?' The questioning continued.

'I have heard great reports about the players who will represent New South Wales and am very much looking forward to seeing them match their skills against our boys.'

James Giltinan stepped forward and raised his hands 'Thank you gentlemen, that's all for now.'

As the two businessmen turned away from the throng a voice shouted, 'Is it true you are taking Dally with you to the old country?'

James Giltinan whispered, 'Keep going Albert, don't turn around whatever you do.'

Five days later, on the 13th August 1907, the two teams made history as they stepped out onto the Royal Agricultural Society Showground in front of over 20,000 excited spectators. As Messrs Giltinan, Trumper and Hoyle took their seats in the stand next to Albert Baskerville the sun was shining on a perfect day for playing rugby football. James Giltinan's delight was obvious. 'The gods are with us Albert. The sun is certainly shining on the righteous today.' He pointed to the crowd of reporters in the specially allocated area near the half-way line. 'Let's hope that the teams put on a spectacle to convince the doubters about our new league.'

'Are you pleased with the attendance James; how many were you hoping for?' asked Albert.

'Pleased? Albert we are delighted! We had hoped for around twelve thousand, but I think there must be close on twenty thousand here today.'

'Is that typical of the reaction of the general public to the new league over here James?' Albert enquired.

'The general public – unlike certain sections of the press – have a very open mind. All they want is to be entertained, they have no bias against professionalism whatsoever. I wish I could say the same about' he paused for a moment and rubbed his chin with his right hand 'let's say the more conservative elements of the press and the establishment as a whole.'

'I know what you mean James – we have experienced exactly the same reaction to the tour in New Zealand. I imagine our forerunners in the Northern Union will have come up against the same resistance in the Old Country back in 1895.'

The referee blew his whistle to signal the start of the very first professional game of football on Australian soil and a great cheer went up from the spectators.

The touring New Zealanders eventually ran out winners by 12 points to 8 in a closely fought encounter and the general opinion was that the game had been a success. The Sydney press decided that Richard Wynyard of New Zealand and Dally Messenger for the home team were the stand-out performers.

A follow up game took place four days later at the same ground and once more the tourists were triumphant, this time by 19 points to 5. The final game of the series was a closer affair but again the tourists prevailed, this time by 5 points to 3. This final game of the series was Dally Messenger's first game as captain of New South Wales and he once again marked it with a sparkling performance.

Shortly after the final game it was announced that Messenger would be joining the touring party for the trip to Great Britain.

After the third game of the series James Giltinan and Albert met to divide up the profits. 'Well Albert we gave you and your team a guarantee of £500 for the three games but I'm pleased to say that the attendances exceeded our expectations and we are able to increase your share to £600.'

'That's wonderful news James, the money will be very welcome as our costs for the tour are higher at the start. Along with the money collected from each of the players we should have enough now to keep us solvent until the money starts to come in from the games against the teams of the Northern Union. But tell me James how has the New South Wales Rugby League done from our three-match series?'

'We've done very nicely from a financial point of view Albert. Your visit has come at just the right time. The funds we've raised will help us to launch the new league when the season begins next year. But more important, even than the money, is the profile that the games have given us. The fans have loved it and most of the papers are coming around to supporting us, and, as we both know, getting the press on your side can make the difference between success and failure.'

There was a large crowd of well-wishers at the docks to wave the tourists on their way to the Old Country and prominent amongst them was James Giltinan who made his way to shake hands once more with Albert Baskerville.

Albert Baskerville (left) in his tour boater and jacket. How amazing that such a young man could have such an impact.

'Thanks again Albert, you and your team-mates will go down in history for the part you have played in helping us launch professional rugby in

New South Wales. You travel with all our good wishes, Victor and Henry would have liked to have been here but business pressure for Victor and politics for Herbert have prevented them being here.'

'Well thank you too James and please pass on our good wishes to your colleagues. Maybe we'll call in on our way back and play you again but this time under Northern Union rules.'

'That's a great idea Albert. On a different matter I heard that you've had word from the New Zealand Rugby Union, what did they have to say, I don't suppose they were wishing you good luck and God speed?'

'Far from it, James. We've all been banned by them for life, so there's no turning back now.'

The ships whistle blew, followed by the cry 'All aboard' so the two men shook hands and Albert dashed off and ran up the gang plank.

As James Giltinan waved his new-found friends away on their journey to the other side of the world, he reflected on Albert's idea of a return match under Northern Union rules. By his calculations the touring party should be returning around the time when the first matches of the New South Wales Rugby League were taking place. A series of matches against the returning tourists would attract a lot of interest and generate more funds for the fledgling league. He made a mental note to discuss the idea with Victor Trumper and Herbert Hoyle.

CHAPTER 7 – YOUNG HAROLD'S PROGRESS

1906 Huddersfield

Joe Clifford was taking nothing for granted. He wanted to make sure that his new signing was introduced to the Huddersfield trainer, Arthur Bennett, and his new teammates in the right way. With this in mind he had arranged to meet Harold at the railway station in Huddersfield and travel with him by tram to the ground at Fartown.

They arrived at the ground before the rest of the players so that Joe Clifford could, not only introduce the new signing, but also to speak to the trainer about Harold's request for an early run out with the first team. He asked the young man to wait outside the changing room and went inside.

Arthur Bennett had been a stalwart of the Huddersfield club for many years. Initially as a player, before taking up his present position three years ago after his playing days were over. He was a typical, bluff, no nonsense Yorkshireman who would call a spade a spade. His reaction to Harold's request for a place in the first team was both typical and predictable.

'Cocky little bugger isn't he. And what if I don't think

he's ready for playing in't first team?'

'I have explained to him that you will want to have a look at him in training before committing to selecting him for the first team.' Joe Clifford re-assured the trainer. 'But I'm confident that you'll like what you see.'

'And how old did you say the lad is?'

'Fifteen, going on sixteen actually. But he's very mature for his age – both physically and in the way that he handles himself.'

'Aye well bring the lad in we can't leave him standing out there all night can we.'

Joe Clifford opened the changing room door and indicated for Harold to come in. 'Right Harold, this gentleman is our trainer Mr Bennett.'

Harold strode confidently forward and shook hands with Mr Bennett. 'I'm very pleased to make your acquaintance Mr Bennett.'

Arthur Bennett turned to Joe Clifford, 'Well you weren't exaggerating when you said he was a big lad for his age.' He then turned back to speak to Harold 'Mr Clifford here, reckons you're keen to have a run out wi' the first team young man.'

'Aye Mr Bennett, I am that.'

'D'you think you'll be able to hold yer own wi' these 'ere professionals then 'Arold?'

'Well I've been playing open age wi' Underbank and I've held me own. And that includes a game against your second team.'

'That's true Arthur Joe Clifford jumped in 'I was at that game and that's when I first spotted Harold's talent. I've been monitoring his progress ever since.'

'This is what we'll do then 'Arold. We've two training sessions this week so we'll see how you get on wi' the other lads and make a decision after training on Thursday. If you can show me, and the other selectors, that you're ready then you'll be in the team.'

At this point the other players began to arrive and Harold was introduced to them all individually.

When the team sheet for Saturday's match against Bramley was pinned up on the dressing room wall after training on Thursday night there it was, centre three-quarter – Harold Wagstaff. Harold couldn't wait to get home and tell his father and brother that he was playing for the first team.

There was another surprise for the young footballer when he arrived home from work on Friday evening. His father was sat at the table reading Friday's edition of the Huddersfield Daily Examiner. 'Now then lad, it seems you're a record breaker already.' Harold's brother Norman was also there.

'How come, father?'

'Well according to the reporter in th'Examiner, you're the youngest ever player to play in't first team in a Northern Union game. He's even gone to the trouble of calculating your exact age on Saturday. Apparently, yer'll be 15 years and 175 days old.'

'Well I never. I just hope I don't let any of me new teammates down.'

'Ah yer'll do well enough 'Arold. If I know you, you'll score a try on your first match' chimed Norman. 'And we'll be there to cheer you on won't we father.'

'Wouldn't miss it for the world lad. When I see you walk out on that pitch wearing the claret and gold, I'll be fair proud.'

Saturday 10th November 1906 marked the professional debut of young Harold Wagstaff. Few people in the crowd at Barley Mow, the home ground of Bramley, could have imagined the impact that the young man who was making his debut that day would have during his illustrious career.

Andrew Wagstaff and his son Norman arrived early at the ground and made their way to a position close to the half-way line. As the kick-off time approached Andrew Wagstaff confided in his son, 'Eeh Norman, the last time I was so nervous was when I married your mother, God rest her soul. I hope the lad is controlling his nerves better than me.'

'Don't worry yourself Father. Our 'Arold will be fine. He may be only fifteen years old, but he's got an old head on those young shoulders tha' knows.'

'Aye, well he'll need his wits about him judging by the size of yon chap he's up against' Andrew Wagstaff pointed at the stocky player that Harold would be marking.

'That's Albert Hambrecht father, he's been around for quite some time, and he's laked for Yorkshire a time or two. I fancy our 'Arold will be able to show him a clean pair of heels if he get's a bit of space.'

'It's not what our 'Arold will do to him that's bothering me lad. It's what will happen when yon Hambrecht gets into his stride wi' the ball in his hands that I'm worried about.'

Hambrecht had a smile on his face and was rubbing his hands as he exchanged a few words with one of his teammates as they lined up for the kick-off. 'So, the young lad fancies himself as a professional does he? Just let me have the ball and we'll soon see what he's made of.'

The moment of truth was not long in coming. The game was only five minutes old when the Bramley half back fed a short pass to the burley centre who quickly got into his stride and headed straight for the young debutant. Harold wasn't one to be intimidated and held his ground as Hambrecht ran into him at pace, knocking Harold to the floor. Andrew and Norman Wagstaff flinched in unison at the impact, but young Harold hung onto the burly centre's ankles and dragged him to the floor.

As Harold slowly got to his feet a team-mate patted him on the back, 'Well played 'Arold that were a fine tackle, but if you want to finish the game, you'd better tackle him side-on next time'.

Albert Hambrecht was not the only centre who made an impact on the young debutant in the early stages of the game. Jim Davies was Huddersfield's other centre that day and he must have had his doubts about playing alongside such an inexperienced young man. Davies, who would earn a place on the inaugural Northern Union tour of Australasia in 1910, had a reputation for not suffering fools. Early on in the game he created an opening for Harold and sent a bullet like pass out to him. The speed of the pass clearly caught Harold by surprise, the ball was dropped and a try scoring opportunity went begging – much to Davies's annoyance.

As the game progressed the Huddersfield team started to take control and Norman's prediction that his brother would score on his first appearance in the claret and gold proved correct. At the final whistle the score was 28 points to 11 in Huddersfield's favour. As the opposing players shook hands Albert Hambrecht made his way to shake hands with his opposite number. 'Well played young man. I can see that you'll do well in't game. You're a fast learner alright. I thought that first tackle might have put you off, but you soon worked out the best way to tackle, and that was a fine try you scored.'

'Thank you, Mr Hambrecht. I don't think I've ever been hit as hard in my life as that first tackle I made on you. It felt like I'd been hit by a steam roller.'

'Aye, I've tried that approach on a load of young centres in the past and they don't usually come back for more like you did. I'll be watching your progress with interest lad, good luck.'

Rugby is a tough game and no quarter is given during a game, but warfare ends when the final whistle blows and the young debutant and the experienced pro walked off the pitch together having a friendly chat.

Arthur Bennett was waiting for Harold as he entered the dressing room. 'Well played young man, I had my doubts about you up against old Hambrecht there, but you did yourself and the team proud.'

The next person to congratulate him was none other than Joe Clifford. 'Well played Harold, how does it feel to be a true professional?'

'It feels really good Mr Clifford, but I've got a sore shoulder from that first tackle on Albert Hambrecht.'

'Aye I saw that. I wasn't sure if you would get up after that one, but you did. It was a real test of your resolve Harold and you came through with flying colours. I gave a promise to your father that we'd look after you, and not rush you. Our next match is against Halifax, but we'll rest you for that game to give your body a chance to recover and then you will play the week after against Leeds at Fartown. I've spoken to the other selectors and they are all in agreement.'

'Oh, thanks Mr Clifford. I can't wait to play at Fartown, the ground where I've watched my local team play since I was a lad.'

'I've also had a word with Mr Bennett and told him to give you some more coaching on your tackling technique. As I said I made a commitment to your father that we'd look after you and I intend to keep that promise.' Joe Clifford started to walk away and then stopped. He turned around with a big smile on his face, put his hand in his pocket and pulled out a small brown envelope; someone had written 'WAGSTAFF' on the cover. There was a broad smile on Clifford's face as he handed it over to Harold. 'Don't you want this then Harold?'

There was slightly bemused look on Harold's face as he opened the packet to find 25 shillings[14] in it. He looked inquisitively at John Clifford who smiled and said 'It's your wages lad. But don't expect that every week, its only 10 bob[15] if we lose.'

The young player was speechless, he sat staring at the money for a few seconds before stuttering 'Thank you Mr Clifford, I'd better give this to me father to look after.'

To which Joe Clifford responded 'It's your wages lad, you've earned it. It's up to you what you do with it.'

Harold was absolutely buzzing with excitement as he made his way to his father and brother who had stayed behind to wait for him to emerge from the Huddersfield dressing room.

'Well played 'Arold' Norman gave his brother a congratulatory slap on the shoulder. Harold winced with pain. 'Sorry 'Arold I never thought, is that from when the big fella cracked you?'

'Aye it is Norman, I don't think I've ever been hit so hard in a rugby match, or anywhere else for that matter.'

'I was surprised you got back up after that son' Andrew Wagstaff observed. 'But I was very proud when you finally made it to your feet. What did your team-mate say to thee straight afterwards?'

Harold laughed 'He told me not to be so stupid and try not to tackle him head on in future. It was good advice too, I made sure I got him side on from that point. Oh, and Mr Bennett is going to give me some more tips on how to tackle them big fellas like Albert Hambrecht.'

'Aye, I should think so too. If you keep getting hit like that your rugby career will be over before it's even started.'

Harold started to fiddle around in his pocket. 'What the hell's up with you lad, can't you keep still?' chided his father.

Eventually a crumpled up brown envelope appeared 'Here you are father, look after this for me please?'

'What 'ave you got there, little brother' asked Norman.

'It's me wages, there's 25 bob in there, winning pay. Mr Clifford said not to expect that much every week 'cos it's only 10 bob if we lose.'

Andrew Wagstaff took the package from his son, slapped him on his shoulder, bringing another wince from him and said I'll open a bank account for thee on Monday and you can put this away for a rainy day.'

'Thanks father, that'll do nicely.'

'I think we'll all pop up to your uncle's place and let him know how you've got on today and we'll all have drink to celebrate. Me and Norman will have a pint and you can have shandy 'Arold. I think we've all earned it today.' And with that they all set off for the tram back to Huddersfield from where they would catch the train up to Holmfirth.

Joe Clifford proved to be a man of his word and ensured that the young Harold Wagstaff didn't play every week. After making his home debut against Leeds he was left out of the team for a couple of weeks. As the season wore on and Harold's physique developed further and his strength increased, he became a regular member of the team.

At the start of the following season Harold had established himself as one of Huddersfield's first choice centres, so it was with great excitement that he read in the papers about the proposed tour by a team from New Zealand who would play against the teams from the Northern Union. Harold remembered how the previous All Blacks had earned the nickname of the Invincibles and had only lost one game in the entire tour. He also read with interest about the only Australian player in the team and the reputation he had developed for his starring performances as a centre three quarter – the same position as Harold played.

Young Harold would not have to wait long to compete against the tourists. When the programme of games for the tour was published their second game would be against Harold's Huddersfield team. On the 12th October 1907.

When Albert Baskerville's tourists finally arrived in the North of England none of them had ever seen a game played under Northern Union rules. They would have two short weeks to recover from their voyage and prepare for their first game. In this period, they went to watch a local derby between Leeds and Hunslet and undertook a crash course in the Northern Union rules. Their first game on British soil was at Barley Mow against Bramley, a game which they won by 25 points to 6.

The game against Huddersfield was a closer affair and the home team lead by 8 points to 3 at half time. However, the tourists, including Dally Messenger and Lance

Todd, came back strongly in the second half and ran out easy winners by 19 points to 8, in front of a crowd of over 10,000.

After the match Harold was disappointed but not dismayed. The star player on this occasion was Lance Todd the New Zealand half back who would go on to have a great career in the Northern Union playing with Wigan. At the final whistle Harold rushed over to Messenger and Todd who were walking off together and shook hands with them both. Messenger patted Huddersfield's youngest player on the back 'Well done kid, carry on like that and you'll have a great career.'

Although no-one present at the match could have known it at the time, three of the touring team who played that day would later play and win trophies in the Claret and Gold of Huddersfield. Edgar Wrigley initially joined Runcorn before moving to Huddersfield. Con Byrne played with North Sydney in the newly formed New South Wales Rugby League until he signed for Huddersfield and William Trevarthen also took up a contract with the Huddersfield club. Wrigley in particular, would play a key part in the transformation of Huddersfield from a struggling side to a champion one.

The remainder of the 1907/8 season was a period of consolidation for young Harold Wagstaff. The Huddersfield team had been in the doldrums since the advent of professionalism in 1895 but were starting to show signs of improvement and towards the end of the season their form improved significantly. They won six of their last seven league matches running in 229 points whilst only conceding 45. At the end of the season they finished in fifteenth position having won slightly fewer games than they lost. Huddersfield's gradual improvement would continue over the next few seasons as the club would re-cruit international players from Australia as well as New Zealand. Harold had made 24 appearances and scored just 2 tries, one against Hull Kingston Rovers and the other on his return to Bramley.

The 1907/8 season would be a landmark for the Hunslet club who became the first team to win all four trophies available to them in the same season. They beat Halifax by 17 points to nil in the Yorkshire Cup Final and won the Yorkshire League. Victories in the Challenge Cup Final (Hull 14 – 0) and the Championship (Oldham 12 – 2, after a 7 – 7 draw) completed their clean sweep of trophies.

Harold Wagstaff was full of admiration for this out-standing achievement as he chatted with his brother one morning on their way to work. 'Can you believe that Hunslet have won all four cups this year Norman. What a team heh?'

'Aye it'll be a while afore anyone else pulls off that feat 'Arold. Mind you we didn't do too bad against them, when we laked 'em. You played in th'ome match didn't you?'

'I did, we lost 17 -11 that day. But I wasn't in the team that played them at Parkside when we ran 'em really close, I think it was 11-9, or summat like that.' Harold went into one of his dreamy moods. 'D'you think we'll ever win any trophies at Fartown Norman?'

'You never know, maybe one day. We had a decent run at the end of last season didn't we, when we won six out of our last seven league games. You played in most of them didn't you?'

'Actually, Norman I played in the last twelve games of the season. I think we might have won a few more games if we'd had a regular goal kicker. Percy Holroyd did most of the kicking, but he only managed 39 all season.'

'I still think we need a few new players though. We could do with signing up some of Baskerville's players, they had some damn good lakers.'

And so, the Wagstaff brothers dreamed of better times for Huddersfield, little did Norman know how prophetic his suggestion of signing New Zealand's best players would turn out to be.

HAROLD WAGSTAFF.

A hitherto unpublished picture of the famous ex-International in three stages of his brilliant career. 1906, when he commenced playing with Huddersfield; 1914, just before his first visit to Australia; 1925, immediately prior to his retirement.

Three images which scan the professional career of Harold Wagstaff. (Courtesy Huddersfield RL Heritage)

CHAPTER 8 – EVERYTHING TURNS TO GOLD FOR THE ALL BLACKS

August 1907 to June 1908

As Albert Baskerville reached the top of the gang plank he turned and waved to James Giltinan and reflected on a highly successful visit to New South Wales. He had already arranged to meet with the tour's management committee in the ships lounge to undertake a formal review of the tour so far and to make plans for the next stage.

The management committee was made up of players, Jim Gleeson, Duncan McGregor, Massa Johnston, Lance Todd and the team captain 'Bumper' Wright (christened Hercules Richard). The committee was completed by the tour manager, Harry Palmer and, of course, Albert.

'Well, gentlemen I am very pleased to report that not only has the Australian leg of our tour been a success on the field of play, but it has also been a financial success. As you know I had negotiated a guarantee of £500 from

Mr Giltinan and the New South Wales Rugby League. In fact – and this was due mainly to the superb attendance at the first match – we have received £600 for the series of games. Perhaps even more importantly than the financial success, Mr Giltinan and his friends, Messrs Trumper and Hoyle, strongly believe that the tour has provided a very significant benefit to the league and its formal launch next season.' There was a round of applause from the group.

'You will all know that we have also added one more player to the squad; a player of the highest talent, and I might add, one of great commercial value to the tour - Dally Messenger.' Another round of applause was interspersed with cheering.

'How did you manage to pull that off Bert?' asked Bumper Wright.

'It wasn't just me Bumper, I can't take all the credit. Let's just say that Mr Giltinan and his friends have been working on it for some time and I was happy to go along with their proposal.'

'Well either way Dally is going to be a real asset to the team,' Bumper added 'he's already fitted in well with the rest of the lads.'

'Now looking forward' Albert was back in business mode 'we need to give some thought to how we keep the lads fit and happy on our long journey to the Old Country.'

Various suggestions were made and discussed, and it was agreed that there would be daily training sessions on deck and games of cricket would also be organised.

The players, all of whom had contributed £50 to join the tour, would be paid £1 per week and would share equally in any profits made by the tour. Several of the players had toured the Old Country previously with the 1905 All Blacks and they were able to advise the other players on how best to pass the time and keep themselves in good shape during the long voyage.

At a stop-over in Ceylon they were challenged to a game of rugby by the Ceylon Rugby Union, which the tourists won by 33 points to 8. Unfortunately for the Ceylon Rugby Union they were subsequently ostracised by the Amateur All Blacks who refused to play them as they had played against the so called professional All Blacks.

The 'professional' New Zealand All Blacks who became known as the All Golds.

The six weeks journey would take them through the Suez Canal and into the Mediterranean. On many days the temperature was far too hot for any physical exertion but once they had reached the Med the weather freshened up and they could resume their training. Eventually they docked in Marseille where they left their ship, the RMS Orsana, and continued their journey across France to Boulogne by train. A short ferry ride across the channel brought them to Folkestone where they took the train up to London.

Whilst on the ferry across the channel Albert took the opportunity to brief all the squad members on the arrangements in England and the importance of the tour not only to themselves but also to the clubs in the Northern Union.

'When we arrive in Folkestone, we will make our way to the railway station to take the train up to London where we will be met by Mr Arthur Hopkinson, the chairman of the Northern Union and a number of his colleagues. I have been in regular contact with Mr Hopkinson and he has been at great pains to emphasise the importance of the tour to his member clubs. He has, therefore, organised for us to be presented to a number of representatives of the press. It seems the timing of our tour is perfect for them, as it gives them an opportunity to raise the profile of the Northern Union to a national audience. It seems that the growing popularity of Association Football has had a serious impact on the attendances at Northern Union matches. Last season they reduced the number of players from fifteen to thirteen in order to make the game more open and, therefore, more attractive to the spectators. We all, therefore, are ambassadors not just for New Zealand but for the sport as a whole. I'm sure that you will all take your responsibilities seriously both on and off the pitch, starting with our arrival in the great metropolis.'

After the press call was over Mr Hopkinson and his colleagues from the Northern Union entertained the touring party at a formal dinner. The following day they all took the train to Leeds where over 6,000 people were waiting in and around the railway station to greet them.

George Smith was overwhelmed as he spoke to Albert 'I don't remember anything like this reception when I was here with the Invincibles two years ago, we were popular, but this is crazy.'

'Mr Hopkinson tells me that since the breakaway in '95 they've been starved of any international matches' replied Albert. 'That's probably why there are so many here today. Let's hope they come to the games in big numbers too.'

For the first part of the tour Leeds would be the base for the tourists. The tour programme allowed them two weeks for acclimatisation to the cold northern climate and also gave them time to get to grips with the Northern Union rules. When the matches finally began the New Zealanders made a brilliant start by playing four games in ten days and winning them all. Attendances were higher than expected with these first four games alone attracting a combined attendance of 48,000.

Their winning streak was ended by Wakefield Trinity who held them to a 5 points all draw, but this was followed by another four straight wins. The unbeaten run came to an end when a strong Wigan side overcame them by 12 points to 8. Any disappointment about this result was offset by the attendance of 30,000. At this early stage in the tour the financial success of the tour was already guaranteed.

As the winter weather began to bight, the form of the tourists slumped. The cold, muddy conditions clearly didn't suit their free-flowing passing game. Between 13th November and the end of January they won only seven of their twenty-one games with one game drawn. Their form did pick up however as they entered the final few weeks in Britain. Their four wins in a row included the final two test matches against the full Northern Union side and thus they won the test series by two matches to one.

The final match of the British leg of the tour resulted in a 21 points to 10 win against St Helens and was noteworthy insofar as Albert Baskerville made his one and only playing appearance of the British leg of the tour and which he marked by scoring a try.

A number of the squad elected to stay on in England as

they had been tempted by the overtures of some of the English clubs. George Smith became an Oldham player, Lance Todd signed for Wigan, and Joseph Lavery for Leeds. Duncan McGregor opened a sports shop and also agreed to play for Merthyr Tydfil and Jim Gleeson decided to finish his legal studies in London.

Throughout the tour Albert had kept his promise to stay in touch with James Giltinan back in Australia and a number of games had been arranged for the team on their return to Australia.

Albert had hoped to include games in North America on the way home but for some reason they didn't materialise. However, when they left British shores they did so with the thanks of the Northern Union. The tour had been a success on many levels. The paying public had turned up in large numbers and had been entertained by some breath-taking rugby. The profile of the game in Britain had been raised and the tour had also generated a great deal of interest back home in New Zealand. The inclusion of Dally Messenger in the tour party had been a master stroke and had guaranteed extensive coverage in the Sydney newspapers, which in turn helped to keep the imminent launch of the professional game in New South Wales in the public eye.

Young Albert Baskerville's vision of players enjoying the fruits of their labours and sharing in the profits had been realised. Albert had proved to be a shrewd negotiator and had agreed that the tourists would get 70% of all gate receipts with a guarantee of at least £3,000 from the Northern Union. By the time they had completed a second series of games in Australia the players' share of the profits had risen to nearly £300 each, a substantial sum indeed.

On the playing front they had won 19 and drawn 2 of their 35 games in Britain. Although they had lost close fought games with Wales (9 – 8) and England (18 – 16) they had won two of the three test matches against the Northern Union which included the best players from both Wales and England.

It had been a gruelling schedule. The first game had taken place on 9th October at Bramley and the final game was on 22nd February at St. Helens, a period of just over 19 weeks. They had travelled up and down the country from Workington in the North West to Hull in the East and London in the South, along with several visits to Wales.

On board the ship on the way back to Australia, Albert and the tour captain, Bumper Wright, reflected on the success of the tour. 'What do you think then Bert' Bumper started the conversation. 'Has it reached your expectations?'

'It's gone way beyond anything I could have hoped for Bumper. The reception in the Old Country has been fantastic, we've been welcomed wherever we went, and the fans turned out in big numbers. The players have been fantastic; I was worried about how they would adapt to the new rules but the fact that we went unbeaten in our first nine games proves that that wasn't a problem. In fact, the new rules really suited our style of play and I think they'll go down well back home.' Albert paused for a moment, 'You're a bit closer to the players than me Bumper, how do you think they feel about the tour?'

'Well, everybody is shattered but I think they've all enjoyed the footy. Quite a few of the lads have been a bit homesick and the weather hasn't always been kind has it?'

'I take your point about the tiring schedule, but the lads will have plenty of time to rest up on the way home. But we mustn't forget that we've got some more important games to come, back in Australia, so we'll need to get them all back in shape before we land in Sydney.'

'We're going to be a bit short in the backs what with George, Lance and Jim staying behind in England and I guess Dally will be playing for the Aussies won't he?'

'That's right, we'll see if we can draft some more lads in from back home. Who do you think would fit in well Bumper?'

'I reckon Jim Barber from Wellington would be a good fit if he's available. He's a good scrum half and he's versatile. I think he's played in quite a few of the back positions.'

'Fair enough, I'll get onto that when we make land and see if Jim's interested.'

'You've kept in touch with Mr Giltinan and the other guys in Australia haven't you; do you know how the preparations for the new league are going over there, Albert?'

'From what I've heard its going really well Bumper. If the voyage is on schedule, we should be there for the first round of the new league, so that should be interesting. There's quite a bit of interest up in Queensland as well so I think James – Mr Giltinan – is hoping to arrange some games for us up in Brisbane. It will mean a bit more travelling for the lads I'm afraid.'

'Oh don't worry Albert I'm sure the lads will be up for it once we get there.'

CHAPTER 9 – ALBERT BASKERVILLE'S FINEST HOUR

When the tourists finally landed in Sydney on 9th April 1908 James Giltinan was there at the dock side to welcome them. As he shook hands with Albert he said 'Congratulations Albert. From what I hear your tour of the Old Country has been a resounding success. We've been following your exploits over here with great interest.'

'Well thank you James, it's really good to get back and feel the warmth of the Southern Hemisphere sun. England was a great experience but the weather over there, particularly in winter, was something else.'

'As ever Albert your timing is impeccable. The new season starts in two weeks and we have eight confirmed teams. They are all going to be needing some intensive coaching in the new rules, so I thought we could get your lads to spread out amongst the teams and help them to become familiar with the new rules and how best to play under them.'

'I'm sure the lads will look forward to that. It's difficult to keep fit on board a ship and we're all a bit out of condition after the long voyage so running out with the new teams will be good for us. What about our playing schedule James, we'd all like to see the first round of the new league before setting off on our travels'.

'I thought that might be the case Albert, so I've arranged for you to stay in Sydney until after the first round then you've got a couple of games up in Newcastle, before coming back to Sydney for a couple of games against a New South Wales select and then you'll play the first ever rugby league test match in Australia.'

'I thought you said we'd be playing some games up in Queensland James, is that still part of the plan?'

'Yes, it certainly is Albert. We're arranging four more games up in Brisbane including a second test match. Your programme finishes with a third test match back in Sydney on 6th June'.

Albert's surprise at the schedule was evident. 'Well that's quite a programme James. You're certainly keeping us busy.'

'Well I can't emphasise too much the importance of these games for our young sport. The games you played here last year, your exploits in the Old Country and the launch of the new league have generated lots of interest. Now it's important that we maintain that level of excitement and we think the programme of games we have arranged will do just that and bring in the spectators. I know we are working you guys hard, but, as you found last time you were here you will be rewarded handsomely for your efforts.'

And so, the professional All Blacks undertook the third and final stage of their world tour. There would be ten more games in just over six weeks.

Jim Barber was approached and was excited at the prospect of joining the squad, whilst Dally Messenger left the squad, as expected, and reverted back to playing for his home state and country.

The team travelled up to Newcastle for the first leg of the Australian tour, still rusty from their long journey. A team from Newcastle was competing in the new Sydney based league, playing all their games in Sydney so there had never been a game played under Northern Union rules in the Newcastle area. The tourists first game was actually played under traditional rugby union rules and ended in a convincing win for the tourists by 53 points to 6. The second game, which took place three days later on 25th April 1908, was therefore the first ever game of Rugby League played in Newcastle and ended in another big win for the tourists, this time by 37 points to 8.

When the New Zealand tourists returned to Sydney, they played two games against New South Wales who, as expected, included their former All Black colleague Dally Messenger in their side. The two games were open and entertaining and both were won by the New South Wales team. The first match by 18 points to 10 and the second by 13 points to 10. Although they lost the two matches it was clear that the New Zealanders were getting back to full fitness and their sharpness was returning in time for the first test.

On 9th May 1908 Albert Baskerville made his test debut for the All Blacks. It was the first Test match to take place under Northern Union rules between the southern hemisphere nations. Albert marked his test debut by being one of the try scorers for the All Blacks as they won a tight encounter by 11 points to 10. Lining up on the Australian side was Dally Messenger, but for once he did not have his goalkicking boots on, managing only two successful kicks from a staggering fourteen attempts against his former colleagues. The Australian team included three players from Queensland in their team and there was some debate in the press as to whether that had improved the team or not.

Albert's test debut was the high point of his playing career and he was applauded for his display and fully deserved his try. As the team boarded the steamer that would take them up the coast to Brisbane for the Queensland leg of the tour Albert was in buoyant mood. As he sat on the ship's deck chatting with the tour manager, Harry Palmer, he was congratulated on his achievements.

'That was a great victory over the Aussies Bert' Harry Palmer began. 'What did it feel like to make your debut in such an important game: one that you had done so much to make possible?'

'To be honest Harry, I was nervous as hell. I didn't want to let the lads down. As you know I haven't played that much recently with all the administration and organising. If we hadn't lost so many backs, what with the lads staying over in England and then losing Dally, I probably wouldn't have played.'

Harry continued, 'It was a proud moment for all of us, something that only twelve months ago we couldn't have imagined. A professional All Blacks team playing the best of Australia under Northern Union rules'. He paused before adding 'And it's pretty much all down to you Bert.'

'It's nice of you to say that Harry but I only played a small part. People like James Giltinan and Victor Trumper did all the groundwork here in Australia. And don't forget the Northern Union, they were the ones who gave us the opportunity to go over there and learn their game. It's the tour that put international rugby league in the spotlight but without the Northern Union's support it would never have happened.'

'And the works not finished yet is it Bert? Here we are on another trip to spread the word and show the good people of Queensland what rugby league is all about.'

'We live in exciting times Harry. Another day another challenge. To think that a year ago I was sat in the Wellington post office weighing parcels to go back to the Old Country. Now I've travelled around the world, organised the first ever professional rugby tour and scored a try on my international debut. It doesn't get much better.'

So, the 25-year-old Albert Henry Baskerville was riding the crest of a wave, living the dream. He had been instrumental in the creation of international rugby league in both Britain and Australia. How cruel life can be as the healthy young man was struck down on the voyage to Brisbane with pneumonia.

On arrival at Brisbane he was admitted to hospital where he died a few days later on 20th May 1908. Harry Palmer and players representing each New Zealand state accompanied his body back to New Zealand. There was little appetite in the All Blacks squad to continue the tour but after due consideration it was agreed that Bert would have wanted them to fulfil their commitments to the Australian organisers.

On the day that Albert Baskerville died the tourist beat Brisbane by 43 points to 10 having previously beaten Queensland by 34 points to 12 three days earlier. Three days after Albert's death the tourists were lining up once more to meet a Queensland team who had been strengthened by the inclusion of none other than Dally Messenger. Messenger would put in a man of the match performance contributing nine points in a twelve points all draw. Messenger had therefore played international football for Australia at rugby union, New Zealand and Australia under Northern Union rules as well as state football for New South Wales in both codes and now Queensland under Northern Union rules.

The Sydney Herald, on 27th May, printed a short article marking Albert's death in which it stated *'he practically originated the rugby league movement in Australasia'*. A fitting epitaph indeed.

Although they were still mourning the loss of their charismatic organiser and player the All Blacks put on an outstanding display to beat Australia convincingly in the second test match on 30th May by 24 points to 12 to seal the series win. Albert Baskerville would have been proud.

The touring side returned to Sydney for the final test match, and last match of their marathon round the world tour, in which Australia had their first ever test match victory by 14 points to 9.

When the team returned to New Zealand a memorial match was organised to raise funds for Albert's widowed mother. The match, which was the first ever played under Northern Union rules in New Zealand, raised over £300.

And so, the first tour to take place under Northern Union rules finished on a tragic note. It is, however, impossible to overestimate the significance of the tour to the sport of rugby league in both hemispheres. The two separate visits by the professional All Blacks to Australia attracted a level of interest which helped to launch the fledgling sport in both New South Wales and Queensland. Their visit to Britain provided a welcome boost to the Northern Union at a time when its core support was being eroded by the increase in popularity of professional Association Football. The tour also provided a blueprint for future tours. James Giltinan would finance and lead the first Australian tour to the British Isles in 1908 and the Northern Union would send a squad to visit Australia and New Zealand in 1910. In fact, cross hemisphere tours became regular events in the run up to the first world war with Australia touring again in 1912 and the Northern Union reciprocating in 1914. But more of that later...

CHAPTER 10 – YOUNG WAGSTAFF BREAKS MORE RECORDS

1908 Yorkshire

In his first two seasons playing professionally Harold Wagstaff made a total of 47 appearances. The 1908 – 09 season was to be another landmark season for the young Yorkshireman as he would set two more records. When he was selected to represent Yorkshire in a County Championship game against Cumberland on 17 October 1908 he would be just 17 years and 151 days old. The game, which was played on his home pitch at Fartown, ended in a 30 points to nil win for Yorkshire. Harold must have performed well as he was selected to play against Lancashire two weeks later at Salford. A few weeks later he became the youngest person ever to be selected for his country when, at the age of 17 years and 228 days he was selected, along with his clubmate Percy Holroyd to play for the Northern Union against the touring Australians on 2nd January 1909. Wagstaff and Holroyd helped their team to record a 14 points to 9 victory, with Holroyd scoring the winning try. Coincidently this match was also played at Huddersfield's own ground in front of 7,000 spectators.

Appearing for the Australians that day was another young player who would subsequently rise to fame with the Huddersfield team. The player in question was Albert Aaron Rosenfeld, who at the time was a stand off half but he would later become a record breaking winger when he signed for Huddersfield.

Young Harold Wagstaff wears his York-shire kit with pride. (Courtesy Hudders-field RL Heritage).

The 1908 – 09 season would see Huddersfield improve their final position in the league from 15th the previous season to 5th, a major step forward. It marked the start of a steady improvement as the club started to enhance its playing roster with some exciting players, both British and foreign.

That season's Australian tour was far from successful from both a playing and financial perspective. A number of factors conspired to badly affect the attendances. There was a long running strike of mill workers in Lancashire and Yorkshire which caused genuine hardship for the mill workers and severely restricted attendances. To this can be added one of the worst winters in living memory. The tourists managed only 17 wins and 6 draws from their punishing 45 match schedule including a 2 – nil defeat in the Ashes test series. Worse still the financial side was so perilous that the players £1 per week allowance was halved and the Northern Union had to pay

for the touring party's transport back home. James Giltinan, the key man behind the professional movement in
Australia had underwritten the tour and he would face
bankruptcy on his return home. The Northern Union's
decision to use the three test matches to promote the
sport outside it's heartland backfired and the attendances were disappointing. The games in London and Birmingham attracted only 11,000 people, but 22,000 did
attend the Newcastle game.

The 1909 – 10 season promised to be an exciting one
for Harold. There were strong rumours that the Northern
Union would undertake its first ever tour to the southern
hemisphere at the end of the season. The touring squad
was likely to be around 25 or 26 players and although
Harold was not the first choice centre his selection for
the game against the Australian tourists demonstrated
that the selectors had him in their minds.

Although the Northern Union was regarded as a professional league the players all had jobs outside rugby. The
average hours worked for manual workers was around 50
per week. Players would attend training sessions twice
a week with a game at the weekend. The playing season
was a long one too. The 34 league games would be added
to by games in the Yorkshire or Lancashire cup and the
Challenge Cup. The successful clubs could easily play 40
or more games in a season. The top players would be
selected to represent their county in the inter county
championship games and if there was a touring team a
couple more games could be added.

The summer then offered a time for recharging batteries. The most common forms of relaxing hobbies in
the North of England in the early twentieth century included crown green bowls and pigeon racing.

Harold Wagstaff had no time for these relaxing pursuits he had one thing on his mind – preparing himself for the next football season. Although he was a naturally fit person he was not prepared to sit back and take it easy over the summer months. He would take advantage of the long summer evenings to go for runs in the hills around his home village of Underbank, stopping from time to time to take in the rugged beauty of the Yorkshire hills.

Harold's brother Norman had by this time recovered from his injury and he would accompany his younger brother from time to time on their country runs. Harold was, of course, by far the fitter of the two of them and would stop at the top of the hills and wait for his brother to catch up.

'Come on Norman, you can do it. I haven't got all day to wait for you' he would shout encouragement to his elder brother.

Puffing and panting a few minutes later Norman would arrive. After a few minutes recovering his breath Norman would complain 'If you're so bloody desperate to go on, leave me behind and I'll see you back at th'ouse.'

'It's alright Norman I were only joking. Waiting for me older brother gives me a chance to sit and take in the view up here – it's grand.'

Norman had recovered somewhat 'I don't remember you doing all this running last summer 'Arold and you did alright last season didn't you.' Norman gulped in some more air. 'You made it into the Yorkshire team and then you played for the Northern Union team an'all.'

'Aye Norman I did, and I'll tell thee summat else. Playing in them games has made me want to play more.' Harold continued to gaze at the stunning views over Holmfirth, the mill chimneys just seemed to add to the beauty. 'Hey, have you heard the rumours about the Northern Union doing a tour to Australia and New Zealand?'

'It's just paper talk at the minute though in't it, there's nothing definite' replied Norman.

'That's as maybe Norman, but if there's a chance of a team going down under then I'd love to be on the boat with 'em.'

'You've done really well to get in't Yorkshire team at your age 'Arold but there's some bloody good lakers in't Northern Union team, what with James Lomas at Salford and Bert Jenkins at Wigan, not to mention Joe Riley over at Halifax.'

'Aye I know that Norman, and you're right they are the first choice centres. I just want to give me sen the best chance to catch their eye. If I can get into the Yorkshire team again and play well, I'll be in with a chance wont I?'

'Right enough 'Arold but I don't want you to be disappointed. You're not twenty yet, there's plenty of time for you and there'll most likely be other tours to Australia in the future.'

Harold knew that his elder brother was talking sense, but it didn't stop him dreaming. After a few minutes thinking it over he said 'Alright Norman, I get the message. Now see if you can keep up with me on the way down.'

Harold set off at break-neck speed down the steep hill towards home. Norman knew he had no chance of staying with him and shouted 'Tell father to put some hot water on for me when you get back.'

Harold's commitment to his fitness didn't waver and he continued working on it throughout the summer and was excited as the new season approached.

Huddersfield's first game of the season was at Bramley,

the scene of Harold's debut almost three years earlier. As expected, the game resulted in a comfortable win for Huddersfield. During the game Harold picked up a graze on his knee. He played in the next two wins against Bradford Northern and Rochdale but the graze had turned septic and blood poisoning set in. At one point Harold's temperature shot up and he was rushed to hospital and for a while his life was in the balance. Thankfully he recovered; but worse was to follow as Harold then contracted diptheria which resulted in him being admitted to the isolation hospital at Seacroft on the outskirts of Leeds.

Due to the infectious nature of diptheria Harold was not allowed visitors whilst in hospital so he had to settle for keeping in touch with his team's fortunes from the newspapers. Ironically whilst Harold was a patient at Seacroft the Huddersfield team enjoyed their first ever trophy success since the formation of the Northern Union in 1895. Wins against Hull Kingston Rovers, Hunslet and Halifax in the early rounds of the Yorkshire Cup were followed by a 21 points to nil win against Batley in the final which was played at Headingley, Leeds.

Harold was eventually discharged from hospital and was able to resume training in January. By this time the rumoured Northern Union tour of Australasia had been confirmed and Harold was determined to make a late bid for inclusion in the tour party.

Huddersfield's league form from the previous season was continuing. The team had been strengthened by the signings of Albert Rosenfeld and Edgar Wrigley along with a promising loose forward from Cumberland named Douglas Clark.

Harold threw himself into training in an attempt to regain his place in the Huddersfield team and then hope-fully convince the tour selectors that he was worthy of a place in the squad for the tour. His brother Norman and his father Andrew urged a more cautious approach.

'Now then lad, don't be in such a rush. You've just re-covered from a serious illness' his father pointed out. 'You need to build your fitness up gradually.'

'Fathers right 'Arold. We were all very worried when they said you had that there diphtheria thing. It's a killer y'know.'

'Aye but I'm right as rain now. And look how well Far-town are doing without me. If I don't get me sen fit then I won't get into the first team, never mind get picked for the tour.'

His father continued 'I know you're desperate to get back on't field of play, but you need to do it gradual lad. You're always in too big a hurry. Slow down, it's for your own good.'

'I suppose you're both right, but I'd really set me heart on making the tour.'

'Don't worry lad there'll be other tours and you're still a young lad.' His father gave him a sympathetic pat on the shoulder and the matter was closed.

In the end the selectors didn't get chance to consider Harold Wagstaff for the tour as Harold's bad luck with in-juries struck again. He sustained a leg injury in training before he even got back into the Huddersfield team. The injury would prevent him from playing until the end of March, by which time the tour party had already been selected. He was able to make two more appearances for Huddersfield helping them to wins against Leigh and Keighley which enabled them to finish in joint seventh position in the league, two places lower than the previous year but their success in the Yorkshire Cup signalled the start of a period of success.

As soon as he was discharged from hospital Harold couldn't wait to see his team-mates in action. He went to see as many of their matches as possible including away matches. Huddersfield had been drawn in the first round of the Challenge Cup against the league leaders, Oldham, who had a star-studded team. Jim Lomas and Albert Avery were England internationals and the team also included an old team-mate of Albert Rosenfeld's.

Sid Deane played the same position as Harold, centre three-quarter, and had toured with the Australian squad on the ill-fated tour of 1908 – 09 alongside Albert Rosenfeld, and they had become good friends.

On the journey to the match Rozzy, as he was then known, approached Harold 'There's a fella playing for Oldham 'Arold that I would like you to meet, so don't go rushing off after the game will you.'

'And who would that be then Rozzy?'

'It's their Aussie centre Sid Deane, I toured with him a couple of years back. He's a solid guy 'Arold, I think you'll like him a lot. You never know you might even play against him in the Ashes one day.'

'Oh yeh, I remember him from the tour. He's the one they call Snowy isn't he.'

'Yes, that's right, on account of his blond hair.'

'You Aussies really like to give each other nicknames don't you Rozzy. What with Dally Messenger, Pony Halloway and Snowy Deane.'

'I'd never thought of it like that Waggy. But now I come to think about it you're right. I suppose it's a sign of friendship or something like that.' Albert Rosenfeld had a cheeky grin as he placed extra emphasis on Harold's nickname.

The 1908 /9 Australian touring squad. Sid Deane is third from right on the back row.

The 26th February 1910 was a wet and miserable day in Oldham and in a tight game Huddersfield managed to overcome their illustrious rivals by 2 points to nil. Jack Bartholomew scoring the only goal of the match.

As the teams trouped off the field, covered in mud, you could hardly tell which side was which, never mind the individual players but Harold had a sharp eye. As the rival teams were shaking hands he saw Rozzy put his arm around Sid Deane and they exchanged a few words.

Harold waited patiently in the warmth of the club bar until the players had washed and dressed. Sid Deane came into the lounge before Rozzy and looked around the room. He made his way over to Harold and held out his right hand 'You must be the young man that Rozzy has been telling me all about. How do you do I'm Sid Deane.'

Harold rose to his feet and was a little apprehensive 'I'm pleased to make your acquaintance Mr Deane.'

'Now cut the formalities Harold, nobody calls me Mr it's Sid or Snowy to my friends and any friend of Albert

Rosenfeld's is a friend of mine.'

Rozzy eventually entered the lounge and rushed over to the pair who were already chatting away merrily. 'I see you two have met then.'

'Late as usual Rozzy!' Sid admonished his friend in a good-natured way and turned to Harold. 'D'you know Harold when we toured in 08, Rozzy was always the last out of the changing rooms after the game.'

'Well as you can see Sid, he hasn't changed much' and the three players laughed.

'I was just asking Sid here, about the start of professionalism in Australia. I didn't realise that he was one of the first players to join the professional movement.'

'Yeh, that's right Harold. I was actually present at the School of Arts when we formed the North Sydney rugby league team. And I played for North's in the first round of games on 20th April 1908.'

'That must have been a very exciting time when things were starting to fall into place for the professional game.'

'Yeh it was – but it wasn't all plain sailing Harold. There was a lot of pressure from the New South Wales Rugby Union. And most of the papers were against us at first. Y'know it was that tour by Albert Baskerville that really helped us to win the press over. What a shame it was when he died so suddenly at the end of the tour. Albert Baskerville along with Giltinan, Trumper and Hoyle – they were the real heroes. Our tour, the one me and Rozzy were on, was a financial disaster and ruined Giltinan. It was a great shame, the fella didn't deserve that.'

'I just hope the Northern Union tour to Australia doesn't go the same way' Harold responded.

'Ah there's no chance of that Harold. The people back home will flock to the games in their thousands like they did when Baskerville came. They love their rugby league and the weather shouldn't be a problem over there. Not like that winter we toured, god it was awful wasn't it Rozzy.'

'Awful doesn't do it justice – it was far worse than that.'

Harold continued the good natured banter, 'And yet you guys signed up to play over here in our lovely winters, you must be mad.'

'I can't speak for Rozzy but for me the offer I got from Oldham was too good to turn down. Yeh the money was part of it, but to play over here against your top teams and top players, that's what really sold it to me. That's enough about me Harold, how are you getting on? Rozzy tells me you've had some bad luck this year with injuries, and weren't you in hospital at one point?'

'Aye I was Sid but that's all behind me now. I was hoping to get back playing in January and see if I could catch the selectors eye, but then I got this leg injury. I'm on the mend now but I think it'll be a few more weeks before I get back playing and the touring party will have been picked by then.'

'Ah that's a shame but you're still a kid, how old are you 20, 21? There'll be plenty more chances for you'.

Rozzy interrupted 'He's not even 20 yet, go on 'Arold tell him how old you really are.'

'I'll be 19 in a couple of months.'

The look of surprise on Sid's face was clear to see. 'Well I'll be…. Harold, you look after yourself. Don't rush back until you're fully fit; you have lots of time on your side. And congratulations to your boys they did you proud today.' The three friends shook hands before the two Huddersfield players left for the journey back to Huddersfield.

'Thanks for introducing me Rozzy. You were right he's a great chap isn't he.'

'He certainly is, one of the best. But you listen to what he's telling you. Don't come back until that leg of yours is right.'

Huddersfield's success that season in the Yorkshire Cup was their first in the professional era and it was the start of a love affair that the Huddersfield team would have with the competition. It was, in fact, the start of a sequence of six final appearances in seven seasons of which Huddersfield came out victors on five occasions.

Although Harold did not make the tour party two of his Huddersfield colleagues were selected, Jim Davies the team's Welsh stand-off half would be on the boat to Australia along with Jack Bartholomew a winger who came from Morecambe[16].

Harold would have to settle for following his colleagues' fortunes on the tour through the newspapers.

The 1910 tour was a resounding success and many people rated the Northern Union team which beat Australia in the test series as one of the best teams that had played the Northern Union game. The tour captain was Jimmy Lomas from Oldham who was also regarded as the star performer.

As Harold meticulously followed the exploits of the Northern Union team, he reflected on the last twelve months. How high his hopes had been, and how hard he'd tried to reach peak fitness during the summer months only to be thwarted by an innocent graze to his knee. A graze which nearly cost him his life. He resolved to take the advice of his father and friends and have the summer months off to recharge his batteries. He would wait for the pre-season training sessions and then put everything into preparing himself for the new season.

CHAPTER 11 – HUDDERSFIELD ON THE RISE

September 1910

Huddersfield started the season with high hopes and a home win against Ebbw Vale in which Harold scored a brace of tries was an encouraging start. Their optimism was short lived as they lost five of their next seven games. An away win at Bramley in the first round of the Yorkshire Cup, with Wagstaff again on the score sheet, lifted their spirits. Dewsbury were disposed of in the next round and a home win against Hull KR in the semi-final meant that Huddersfield would defend the cup which they had won the year before. The final was played at Headingley, the scene of their previous victory, but there was to be no repeat as local rivals Wakefield ran out winners by 8 points to 2 and Harold Wagstaff's first appearance in a final ended in disappointment.

Huddersfield's league form had been patchy to say the least, but the team bounced back from their cup final disappointment with a 60 points to 19 win against the mighty Hunslet. Had the tide turned for Wagstaff and his talented team-mates?

The answer was no, as Huddersfield could only manage

one more victory in their next seven games and, as the New Year started, they were languishing in the bottom half of the league. The team had lost to Broughton Rangers on 2nd January but then embarked on a remarkable run of form.

Between 7th January and 4th February they played and won five games without conceding a single point. Starting with a 52 points to nil win against Bramley, wins away to the two Hull clubs and a home win against Leeds followed and finally Ebbw Vale at home were all achieved without conceding a single point. In fact the Huddersfield team won all fifteen of their remaining matches, scoring an amazing 490 points in the process whilst conceding only 49. Wakefield Trinity were the only one of their opponents to make double figures, and they were dispatched 44 points to 13. Harold's contribution for the season was 14 tries and 2 goals in his 25 appearances.

The only blot on this impressive run was a Challenge Cup first round defeat by Wigan by 18 points to 13.

Harold Wagstaff was made captain of Huddersfield in late season, whilst still in his teens. He was by far the youngest captain in the league. Huddersfield's impressive form in the second half of the season gave Wagstaff genuine grounds for optimism as he looked forward to the next season.

Following their final match of the season, a 47 points to 2 victory over the once mighty Broughton Rangers, Harold shared a well-earned pint in his local with his brother.

'That was a fantastic run since the beginning of January, Fartown were unbeatable' Norman beamed.

'Well, apart from losing to Wigan in't first round of the

cup' Harold replied. 'That was a real disappointment; we really fancied ourselves to go all the way to the final and win it.'

'Aye but Wigan did finish top of the league didn't they, so there's no shame in that 'Arold. Aren't you proud of what the teams achieved this year?'

'We've achieved nowt Norman' Harold chided his brother. 'We lost to Wakefield in't Yorkshire Cup and finished seventh in the league. You're right we did play well in the second half of the season, but we were all over the shop up to then. The good news is we're developing a good squad full of talented players. We've probably got the quickest backs in the league, with Rozzie, Kitchen, Wrigley and now Stan Moorhouse is coming on as well. That's why we scored so many tries last season, somebody told me it was about 177. That's a lot more than Wigan and like you said they finished top of the table. What was really good about the second half of last season is how good our defence was. The two New Zealanders, Con Byrne and Bill Trevarthen, have made a big difference and Douglas Clark is about the strongest man I've ever played with or against. D'you know Duggie told me he doesn't use all his strength most of the time, he's worried he might hurt somebody if he did.'

'That doesn't surprise me, I've seen him do some amazing things on the pitch and he's a top wrestler as well isn't he?'

'Aye he is' Harold agreed, but he was impatient to get back to his rant. 'So, if we've got the fastest backs in the league and the best forwards, we've just got to do better. We need to take the form we showed in the second half of last season into the new one. If we can do that we'll be challenging for trophies and that's where we should be.'

Who do you reckon will be your biggest challengers 'Arold?'

'I think it will be Wigan and Oldham. Like you said, Wigan finished top of the league, but my mate Snowy Deane's Oldham were too strong for 'em in the championship play off.'

'Wasn't that the first time a team who'd finished top of the league didn't win the championship then 'Arold?'

'Aye that's right Norman. Oldham are going to miss Snowy though, now he's gone back to Australia but they've still got a lot of good players, so I think they'll be there or thereabouts.'

'What about Hunslet 'Arold, they're still a good side aren't they?'

'That's true Norman and then you've got Hull KR and Wakefield to consider. All in all, it's going to be a tough season, but I believe we've got the best all round team, especially now Oldham have lost Snowy.'

'The rugby Fartown played in the second part of the season was as good as anything I've ever seen' added Norman. 'If you can keep that up then the sky's the limit for the team. I just hope you all keep fit and don't have too many injuries.'

'I'll drink to that Norman' said Harold and the two brothers raised their glasses.

Harold was a perfectionist when it came to rugby and spent all his waking hours working out new tactics for making Huddersfield a dominant force in Northern Union rugby. He would discuss these with Arthur Bennett the trainer and they would work on them at their twice weekly training sessions.

September 1911

The 1911 – 12 season was to be the real breakthrough

season for Huddersfield. They took their form from the second half of the previous season into the new season but they did have an early setback. After convincing wins in their first two games against Ebbw Vale and Leeds they travelled to Hunslet with confidence only to be resoundingly beaten by 19 points to nil. Two more home wins followed against Oldham and Warrington before they were held to a 10 all draw at Halifax.

Harold's form must have been good as he was selected for the Northern Union team, along with his team-mate Ben Gronow, to play the first test against the touring side. In order to stimulate the professional game in New Zealand the Northern Union had invited a side made up of both Australian and New Zealanders to send a team over. The first test took place at St James's Park, Newcastle on 8th November and Harold lined up at centre alongside the experienced Bert Jenkins with Ben Gronow in the second row. The tourists proved too strong, however and fully deserved their victory by 19 points to 10.

Meanwhile for Huddersfield the fixtures were coming thick and fast; during October and November the Huddersfield team played and won ten matches, six in the league and four Yorkshire Cup ties.

On 25th November Harold Wagstaff led his Huddersfield team out onto the pitch at Belle Vue, Wakefield in the final of the Yorkshire Cup. Huddersfield were fancied to beat Hull Kingston Rovers and on this occasion they did not disappoint. They put the previous year's loss to Wakefield Trinity behind them and ran out winners by 22 points to 10. It was a proud day for the Wagstaff family as they cheered the young Huddersfield captain as he lifted the Yorkshire Cup. Harold had won his first winners medal, but it would not be his last.

The week after their victory in the Yorkshire Cup final Harold lead his Huddersfield team out against the Australasian touring side, determined to ensure a home victory. On this occasion he was not disappointed, and Huddersfield achieved a convincing 21 points to 7 victory, scoring five tries to one against the strong touring side. It was one of only five games that the tourists would lose in the 35 matches on the tour and a bumper crowd at Fartown of 17,000 enjoyed a thrilling performance by their heroes.

That game took place on 2nd December and was the first of a staggering eight games which Huddersfield played in the month of December, winning seven of them. The sole defeat came at the hands of Hull Kingston Rovers as they exacted revenge on the Fartowners for their Yorkshire Cup final defeat by walloping them by 34 points to 10.

Wagstaff and Gronow retained their places in the Northern Union team for the second test and were joined in the team by Douglas Clark. The game took place on 16th December in Edinburgh and the British team recorded an 11 points all draw with the tourists, including two tries for Harold.

At this time, it was traditional to play not only on Christmas Day but also on Boxing Day. Huddersfield played an away match at Hull on Christmas Day which they won by 21 points to 5 and followed it up a day later with a 62 points to 5 victory at home to local rivals Wakefield Trinity. These mid-winter matches were obviously to the liking of Huddersfield's Australian winger, Rosenfeld, as he scored four tries in the first match and a massive eight tries in the second. It was to be a fantastic season for the Australian speedster as he would rack up a record 76 tries before the season was out.

January 1st brought the final test which was held at the home of Aston Villa in Birmingham. Gronow and Wagstaff were left out of the team which ended in a big win for the tourists by 33 points to 8 to win the series by 2 wins to nil with one game drawn.

Six more league wins followed before Huddersfield had to visit their Lancashire rivals Oldham. Harold was looking forward to the game although he would not be able to renew his friendship with Oldham's Australian centre Sid Deane as he had returned to Australia to resume his career with North Sydney. Oldham had been crowned champions in the previous two seasons and were looking to complete the hat trick, however without their Australian captain their form had been erratic, and they were lying just outside the play off places. This year Huddersfield were genuine championship contenders and this game would be a real test of their credentials. In another close game the home team were victorious by 6 points to 2 to put a temporary stop to Huddersfield's championship challenge.

By this time Huddersfield were in a good position to qualify for the top four play offs and with it the chance to be crowned champions. They were also looking to progress in the Challenge Cup. Comfortable victories in the first two rounds were followed by an away match at Oldham, one of only three teams, at that stage, to have beaten them. Oldham were to prove Huddersfield's bogey team and once more defeated them in a closely fought encounter, eventually winning by 2 points to nil.

Worse was to come for the Fartowners as they lost their next game as well, this time at the hands of local rivals Leeds. Was the Huddersfield juggernaut about to crash? Had the wheels come off?

In this case the answer was a definite no. Huddersfield bounced back and put these two defeats behind them and went on to finish the season with five straight wins to finish top of the league. By finishing in first place they were guaranteed a home match in the play-off semi-final against Hunslet, one of only four teams to have beaten them that season. In the event Huddersfield had no difficulty despatching them by 27 points to 3. The Championship decider would be between Huddersfield and the mighty Wigan and would be played at Thrum Hall the home of Halifax.

The final was played on 4th May and, for the second time that season, Harold Wagstaff and his Huddersfield team would triumph and be presented with the winners medals and a magnificent trophy.

In fact, Huddersfield finished the season with no less than three trophies as they also won the Yorkshire League Championship[17] by virtue of being the highest placed Yorkshire team in the overall championship.

As Harold and his brother Norman sat in their local with pints in hand the conversation inevitably drifted towards the recently completed rugby football season. 'Well 'Arold this time last year you were lamenting a season where the club had won nowt, and now you've got three winners medals. What a difference a year makes eh lad?'

'Aye Norman it certainly feels a lot better, I'll tell thee that' replied Harold.

'What with you being picked for the two test matches as well, scoring two tries in the second one, you must be well satisfied little brother.'

'Aye I am Norman, but only up to a point. The test matches were a great experience. But we did lose the

Ashes and there's no doubt the Aussies and New Zealanders were very good. It's a shame they weren't played in the heartlands though. I reckon with a big crowd yelling us on we could have done better.'

'Aye that were a funny one, why did they play up in Newcastle, Edinburgh and err' he hesitated.

Harold helped him out 'Birmingham. I think the Northern Union were trying to drum up support for the game in places where we don't normally play, or at least that's what they said. But I'd sooner have laked in front of a passionate Yorkshire or Lancashire crowd or even up in Cumberland. There's talk of the Northern Union doing another tour to Australia and New Zealand in 1914. I hope it comes off. I'd really love to be on the boat this time having missed out in 1910. Anyway, going back to Fartown's season I'm still very disappointed we didn't go further in't cup. That defeat at Oldham was hard to take. If we'd beaten them, I reckon we might have won all four cups like Hunslet did a couple of years back'.

'Now that would have been an achievement. You would have gone down in history. What d'you reckon for next year then 'Arold'.

'I hope we can carry on where we left off. Who knows? Maybe if we keep clear of injuries, we might go one better. One thing is for sure Norman.'

'What's that 'Arold?'

'Everybody, every team, every player will be doing their damndest to stop us. So, we'll have to be on top form right from the start and keep it up all year. No room for off days like we had at Oldham last year.'

September 2012

Huddersfield started the next season with the form they had shown at the end of the previous season with five straight wins in September. October brought the traditional Yorkshire Cup first round and Huddersfield were drawn away from home against Hull Kingston Rovers, one of Yorkshire's top teams. On the day they proved to be too strong for Huddersfield and were worthy 11 points to 5 victors.

On the train back to Huddersfield Harold sat with Douglas Clark and reflected on this early season setback. 'It's back to the league next week Duggie, we can't afford another performance like that.'

'Too true 'Arold. The only consolation about being knocked out in the first round is it means we can concentrate on the league and we won't have the usual midweek cup ties to fit in throughout October.'

'We've got some tough games coming up in the next month; Wakefield, Wigan and then we've got this lot again. Like I said we need to be on top of our game or we could lose a few more games.'

'Just look around 'Arold, all the lads are sickened that we've lost today. They're all determined to put this defeat behind us and get on with the league. If I know these lads, they'll get their heads down and work like hell to win every match.'

Douglas Clark's prediction of his team-mates reaction was proven correct. Wakefield Trinity were dispatched the following week and Huddersfield went unbeaten to the end of the year. On the 1st January they stood proudly at the top of the league having played 17 games and won them all. Their winning run was stretched to 19 before their first defeat at the hands of Hull by 8 points to 2. A home game against their bogey team, Oldham, was next up and Huddersfield were beaten again, this time by 10 points to 6.

Normal service was resumed the following week and five wins from the next six matches confirmed Huddersfield's position at the top of the league as they prepared for a tricky away draw in the cup against St Helens. A 19 points to nil victory at Knowsley Road was followed by another away draw this time at Batley who were beaten 8 points to 2. A home win in the next round against Wigan led to a semi-final match with Wakefield Trinity.

By the time the semi final came around Huddersfield had finished their league programme winning 28 of their 32 league matches to finish top of the league with Wigan in second place. Wigan had become the fourth team to beat the Fartowners in the last league match of the season to gain some revenge for their defeat in the Challenge Cup. Hull Kingston Rovers and Dewsbury completed the top four play-off places. Harold's prediction that Oldham would miss the leadership of Sid Deane proved true as they finished well down the table in 11th place.

Huddersfield would have a home draw against Dewsbury in the play-off semi final with Wigan entertaining Hull KR.

Harold and his vice-captain Douglas Clark discussed the challenge ahead. Douglas started the conversation. 'It's make or break time for the lads, two semi-finals in consecutive weeks. We've come a long way this season 'Arold.'

'Aye but we've won nowt yet Duggie. It's Trinity up next in the cup, let's take that one first and then we'll prepare for Dewsbury.'

'They're both good teams so we'll need to be at our best to beat 'em. I fancy Wigan to beat Rovers in the play offs, they gave us a good going over last week and they've got the benefit of a week off while we lake in't cup semi.'

'I'm sure they'd swap places with us though Duggie, and still be in with a chance of the cup and league double. Any road, like I said let's take it one game at a time.'

As it happens the two semi-finals both ended in big wins for the Fartowners who ran in nine tries in the win over Trinity and a further eight tries the week after against Dewsbury. The cup and league double was still very much on. First up would be Warrington in the Cup Final to be played at Headingley. It was a closely fought game in which Stan Moorhouse produced a man of the match performance scoring all Huddersfield's points with three tries in a 9 points to 5 victory to record Huddersfield's first ever win in the Challenge Cup final. Huddersfield owed their victory to some good work by Tommy Gleeson who used his speed to get back and tackle the Warrington forward Skelhorne when he seemed certain to score late on in the game.

Huddersfield's celebrations were put on hold as the Championship final was scheduled for the following week in which they were to play Wigan, who, as expected, had defeated Hull KR in the other semi-final.

Wigan approached the final with confidence having recently beaten the Fartowners convincingly in the league. A close game was expected as the crowd gathered at Belle Vue, the home of Wakefield Trinity, but Huddersfield had other ideas as they ran in seven tries in a 29 points to 2 victory to complete their first ever league and cup double to add to their success in winning the Yorkshire League. Douglas Clark recorded a rare hat trick of tries, Rozzy also added a brace which brought his season's total to 56.

Once again Huddersfield had proven themselves to be the best team in the competition and had been rewarded with three trophies. Wagstaff's goal of leading his team to equal the Hunslet team of 1908 and win all four trophies remained tantalisingly out of their reach.

CHAPTER 12 –
AN INVITATION
TO TOUR
AUSTRALASIA

September 1913

The 1913 – 14 season offered an additional objective for a number of players throughout the Northern Union. The chance to be selected for the Northern Union's second tour of Australia and New Zealand and with it the opportunity to see the world.

Several members of the Huddersfield team had high hopes of taking part in the tour which would take place in the summer of 1914.

Before the season started Harold addressed the full squad. 'Now then lads we've had two very good seasons and won our share of trophies. This season we have the opportunity to carry on that success and write our names in the record books and win more trophies for this wonderful club of ours.' A big cheer went up. When the cheering had subsided Harold continued 'We also have the added incentive of the Northern Union tour of Australia and New Zealand next summer and every one of you – apart from the Aussies that is – is good enough to be on that boat next summer. BUT that will only happen if we keep up our club form for the full season.'

Huddersfield's season followed a similar pattern to the previous two. At the turn of the year they sat top of the league having lost only two games – away at Rochdale and Wigan – and had completed a successful campaign in the Yorkshire Cup beating Bradford Northern in the final by 19 points to 3.

Albert Rosenfeld had started the season in fine form and already had 48 tries to his name and was on course to break his own try scoring record.

Albert Aaron Rosenfeld's record of 80 tries in a season will probably never be beaten. (Courtesy Hudderfield RL Heritage).

The new year started with a draw away at St Helens and defeat at Warrington, but these two setbacks were followed by a string of victories.

Huddersfield started their defence of the Challenge Cup with another record breaking performance. The amateurs of Swinton Park were on the receiving end of a 119 points to 2 defeat. The Huddersfield full back Major Holland had a personal points tally of 39 including 18 successful goal kicks. Rozzy helped himself to seven more tries.

Huddersfield would fail to reach their second successive cup final as they were beaten in the semi-final by a Hull side who included in their ranks Billy Batten who they had signed from Hunslet for a record transfer fee of £600, along with three very talented Australians in Devereux, Gilbert and Darmody. The final score was 11 points to 3 in Hull's favour.

Seven days later Huddersfield took their revenge by running in eleven tries in a 47 -5 victory over the Humbersiders in the league. Huddersfield duly finished top of the league for the third year running and their semifinal opponents were, once again, Hull. This time the Fartowners made no mistake, winning by 23 points to 5. Albert Rosenfeld had already broken his previous record by scoring 80 tries.

Hull's Welsh winger, Alf Francis,was the only player from Hull selected for the tour. Here he is being seen off by well wishers including his 3 Aussie team mates. (Courtesy Mike Baxter)

By this time the Northern Union had selected the players to travel to Australia and New Zealand. Twenty two years old Harold Wagstaff had been given the honour of captaining the tourists and five of his Huddersfield colleagues would join him. Englishmen Douglas Clark, Fred Longstaff and Stan Moorhouse along with Welshmen Johnny Rogers and Jack Chilcott were all included. John Clifford, the Huddersfield chairman, had also been nominated as joint tour manager along with Joe Houghton of Salford. Roles they had fulfilled in the previous tour of 1910.

The tour schedule required the players to set sail for Australia before the Championship final took place and the Huddersfield contingent were granted special dispensation to delay their departure until after the final had been played.

Huddersfield were hot favourites to secure their third championship in a row but their opponents, Salford had achieved second place in the league on merit, based largely on the strength of their defence. Huddersfield's star-studded team and razor-sharp attack were still fancied to be too strong for their opponents. To put this in perspective Salford had only conceded 140 points in their 32 games and Huddersfield had scored 830 points, a massive 500 more than their final opponents.

Huddersfield were odds on to win but Salford's defence proved to be the deciding factor and they were surprise, but worthy, winners in a low scoring match by 5 points to 3. The fact that six of the Huddersfield team were due to leave for Australia immediately after the game was put forward as a possible reason for the team's sub-standard performance in the final. The clear inference being that none of the chosen six wanted to risk an injury which would jeopardise their participation in the tour.

When this point was put to Harold by a reporter after the game Harold's normally calm and controlled way of handling the press disappeared and he became quite agitated. 'I know all these lads and they would never give anything less than their best' he replied. When the reporter pressed Harold to explain why the team had not played to their true potential, he was at a loss to explain. 'At the end of the day we lost because Salford played better than us. That's the top and bottom of it. Instead of criticising us, give the other team the credit for their performance.' And with that he turned away from the reporters and returned to the dressing room.

Later, when Harold had regained his composure he started to reflect on the day's events in a more philosophical way. He could find no obvious reason for their substandard performance. He looked back further, over the last few seasons as the team had risen to the top there had been a number of off days for the team such as the 8 points to 3 defeat by Ebbw Vale in the Challenge Cup in 1910. Games in which Huddersfield were clear favourites to win but they ended in defeat. Then he recalled the 2 points to nil win over Oldham, also in 1910 when Oldham, the reigning champions were hot favourites. His Fartown team that day believed they could pull off a shock victory and worked together as only a true team can to beat a supposedly better team. If his team could do it to other better teams why couldn't other teams do it to them? He decided that the key lessons to be learned were to never under-estimate the opposition when you are favourites and always believe you can win no matter what the odds. A committed team, determined to support each other, can often overcome great odds to achieve their goal. These lessons would serve him well throughout his career and particularly in the forthcoming Ashes series.

The journey to Australia would take six weeks in total and started with a train journey down to Dover where the players would cross the channel by ferry. Another railway journey would take them across the whole of France to the port of Marseille where they would join John Clifford on the MS Otranto. They would then sail east across the Mediterranean before entering the Suez Canal. The first great maritime canal which was opened in 1869 and shortened the sailing time to Australia by over a week. At the southern end of the canal they would enter the Red Sea before crossing the Indian Ocean on their way to Fremantle on the West Coast of Australia. The final leg of their journey would take them to Sydney where they would join the rest of the touring party who had started their journey a full nine days before them. If everything went to plan the Huddersfield contingent would join the rest of the Northern Union tourists just before the first game in Sydney.

Harold was concerned about maintaining the physical fitness of his team-mates during their long journey. He had spoken at length to his great friends and Huddersfield colleagues Albert Rosenfeld and Edgar Wrigley about how they had maintained their fitness and morale on the long journey. Both players had warned him that any physical exercise whilst travelling through the tropics was almost impossible and at least a week on dry land to regain their 'land legs' and improve their fitness before playing any games was essential.

The players had met up with John Clifford, the Huddersfield chairman and co-manager of the Northern Union squad, when they boarded the boat in Marseille. Clifford, who's wife was travelling with him, also had personal experience of the challenges facing the players as he had undertaken the same role four years earlier with the touring party of 1910.

Once the MS Otranto had set sail from Marseille, Harold and John Clifford sat down to plan how to combat the boredom factor and help the players to maintain their fitness on the long journey to the southern hemisphere. It was decided that during the first part of the journey Harold would organise a daily fitness programme which was not too demanding but kept the players in reasonable shape. A sports committee was formed, and competitions arranged to amuse the lads. Once the temperature got too hot the training would be suspended until they reached cooler climes. Deck games would be organised where the players would be joined by members of the crew and passengers. Cricket was a particularly enjoyable distraction. Concerts were a feature of the evening entertainment and the players joined in enthusiastically in the singing.

The players would be allowed shore leave, when the boat dropped anchor in Italy at stops at Naples and Taranto. During the tour, the players were paid an allowance of 10 shillings per week on board ship and 30 shillings per week on shore. In addition to this they would get £10 each when the ship sailed for home and a share of any profits generated by the tour. The married players also had an allowance of 30 shillings a week paid to their wives back in England.

The intensity of the training would increase as they approached Australia in the hope that they would be able to play shortly after their arrival.

John Clifford went through the tourists match schedule with Harold. 'A warm-up game has been scheduled for 24th May when the first group land at Adelaide against a team representing South Australia. We never went to South Australia in 1910 and they've only recently started playing Northern Union rules so I don't know what sort of a team they will put out, but I don't expect them to be too good. Our lads then sail on to Sydney where they have a few days to acclimatise before playing a team called Metropolis. If all goes to plan with our voyage, we should get there in time to watch the game.'

'Exactly who are Metropolis John? I've never heard of them' Harold asked.

'It's a team selected from all the clubs who play in Sydney, so they'll have some very good players to call on. It will be a very difficult game so early in the tour. It took the lads a couple of weeks to get match fit on the last tour, if I remember rightly.'

'Will Dally Messenger be lakin' for them? I'd love to play against him.'

'No, I believe he's retired but his brother Wally might play, he's supposed to be pretty handy too. And Sid Deane, you know the one who captained Oldham when they were in their pomp will most likely be playing.'

'Oh, I know Snowy very well. Rozzy introduced me to him one time when we were playing over at Oldham. He's a sound bloke. We've had a few good tussles me and Snowy. D'you think we'll be there in time to be selected for that game?'

'We should have arrived in Sydney a couple of days before the game, but I doubt that any of the boys will be ready to play after the long journey. As I said Harold, on the last tour it took the lads at least a week to acclimatise and get back to anything like match fitness.'

'If I know these lads, they'll all be desperate for a proper game of football by the time we get there.'

'I take your point Harold but there's a difference between being desperate to play and being READY to play' he put particular emphasis on the word ready. 'I expect the Metropolis team to be mainly made up of players who will be playing in the test series, so they definitely won't be a pushover. If we put players out there that aren't ready, physically ready that is, there's a real danger they'll get injured and that won't help us in the long run Harold.'

'Alright John, you're the boss. I'll leave it to you and Mr

Houghton to pick the team and tell the lads who aren't laking.' He couldn't help but smile at the thought of the probable reaction of some of his Huddersfield colleagues when they were told they wouldn't be playing.

'That game is on the 6th June and then the games come thick and fast. Two days later we play the full New South Wales team which will be virtually the full Australian team.'

'Hells bells, John they're not making it easy for us are they?'

'That's right Harold. The first two games are in Sydney and they say there's going to be a big crowd there for both of them, they're expecting over 40,000 at each game. They're predicting record receipts, which is great for us.'

'They really love their rugby over in Australia, don't they?'

'After that we're on our way North to play Queensland in Brisbane, followed by a game at Ipswich, then back to Brisbane for the first test match before heading back south to play Newcastle.'

'How will we get about for these games John?'

'Well a lot of the games are in or around Sydney, so they won't be a problem; but for the Queensland games we might travel by ship. Australia is a big country Harold. It's over 500 miles from Brisbane to Sydney and the last time I was here there was no direct railway line. Joe is making the travel arrangements, so we'll have to check it with him. The last game at Newcastle is on the 24th June and then we travel back to Sydney for another game against New South Wales. The second test is two days later on the following Monday and the third test is on the following Saturday. All three of those matches are in Sydney. We've even got a game at Bathurst on the Thursday so that's four games in 8 days before we set sail for the New Zealand leg of the tour.'

'Just remind me John. how many games do we play in New Zealand?'

'We've got five games against provincial sides before we play New Zealand in the test match in Auckland on the 1st August. Finally, we head back to Australia for another game against New South Wales.'

'That's quite a schedule, I just hope we don't run into many injuries' added Harold.

'Oh, that reminds me Harold – they have a different rule in Australia about injuries during a game.'

'I remember there was some controversy about that on the 1910 tour wasn't there?'

'Yes, there certainly was Harold. They have this local rule whereby if a player gets injured in the first half of a game, they can bring on a reserve, a substitute if you like. When we heard about this rule in 1910, we cabled the Northern Union to see if we could apply the same rule if we got any injuries, but they flatly refused. Then in the first test Jim Sharrock is injured and we have to play a long period with only 12 men. Jim did manage to come back on half-way through the second half. But if we'd been allowed to replace him we would have done.'

'Will the same rule apply this time John? Have you sorted anything out with the big wigs at the Northern Union?'

'I've had it out with them several times Harold, but I didn't get anywhere. They just flatly refuse – "the use of substitutes is against the rules and open to abuse they say". What, even if the other team is playing by different rules, I said; but I was wasting my time, they just would not budge. They can be very stubborn Harold.' Prophetic words indeed as the tourists would find out to their costs in their very first match in Sydney!

For young men such as Harold Wagstaff, being selected by the Northern Union for the tour of Australasia offered them a unique opportunity to see the world, and Harold was determined to make the most of it. The RMS Otranto would be stopping off at Naples and Taranto in Italy, Port Said in Egypt and finally Colombo, Ceylon en-route to Australia. He was particularly looking forward to the passage through the Suez Canal where they would be able to observe the local life at close quarters.

As the weather got hotter the players all purchased linen suits to keep cool in the hot weather, some of the ladies on-board kindly agreeing to adjust the trousers where necessary to provide a better fit. Most of the players were particularly looking forward to the visit to Port Said as they had heard wonderful stories about this exotic location. Sadly, the place did not live up to their expectations. As soon as they landed, they were faced with a barrage of local traders who were desperate and determined to sell their goods to what they believed were rich passengers. Nevertheless, the players enjoyed a walk around the streets of the bustling town; taking in the scenery and observing the vastly different lifestyle enjoyed by the locals. The players had all been warned not to drink anything whilst on shore as there was a very real risk of the water being contaminated and unsuitable for their more delicate systems.

As Harold pointed out to his friend Douglas Clark 'We've been warned off the water here, but it doesn't seem to bother the locals.'

'Aye you're right 'Arold but that's because their systems are used to it. They must have built up a' he hesitated whilst he searched for the right word.

'An immunity?' suggested Harold.

'That's the word I was looking for, an immunity.'

'The smell out here isn't good either, I've heard they don't have proper sewers here. I'm gagging for a drink Duggie, it's so bloody hot. It almost makes you miss the wind and rain of Huddersfield doesn't it.'

'I wouldn't go so far as to say that 'Arold, but I'm ready to head back to the ship and get a nice cup of tea and sit in the shade for a while.'

'That'll do for me lad, I just hope these ruddy flies don't follow us back onto the ship, they've been having a feast on my flesh.'

Just at that moment Douglas Clark swatted another insect on his left arm as his muscular right arm slapped the unwanted visitor. He carefully picked the squashed insect from his sunburnt left arm. 'That's one less insect to bother us 'Arold. Now let's head back to the ship.'

And with that the two of them made a bee line for the ship, taking care to keep their heads down as they ran the gauntlet of street traders offering their wares. When they finally forced their way through the mass of shouting and heaving bodies and made their way up the gang plank, they were greeted with an ironic cheer from a number of their team-mates who had already returned from their shore visit.

Jack Chilcott was standing at the top of the gang plank waiting to greet them. 'So, did you enjoy your visit to the exotic east 'Arold? I know how much you were looking forward to it.' There was more than a hint of sarcasm in his voice.

'Well Jack, it was quite an experience' came the reply. 'For a minute there I didn't think we'd get through all those traders trying to flog us stuff. I'm glad I had big Duggie with me, they soon stood back when he started to push his way through.'

'It reminded me of market day in Newport, but without the fruit and veg' Jack's sarcasm continued. 'I hope you kept a tight grip on your wallet 'Arold.'

Harold made an instinctive grab for the pocket where he kept his wallet. Panic set in as he realised it wasn't there. 'Oh bloody hell it's gone, the robbing bastards.'

'Now then 'Arold watch your language' Jack Chilcott seemed to be enjoying his captain's misfortune as he continued in his thick welsh accent. 'A good Methodist boy like myself doesn't care for that sort of swearing.'

Harold was getting quite agitated and the rest of his team-mates seemed to be enjoying the spectacle. He couldn't understand why his mates were enjoying his misfortune. Then he saw Jack Chilcott reach behind his own back and produce the missing wallet to a great round of laughter from the onlookers.

Harold was relieved and made a grab for it, but his tormentor playfully pulled the wallet away to more laughter from the spectators. Harold realised he was in for more torment, so he just said 'Alright Jack you look after it for me. It's not as if I need it on the boat' and with that he walked away.

He was followed by Jack who put his arm around him and offered him the wallet with his other hand. Harold had been 'had' once, so he was in no mood to play Jack's game a second time, so he just carried on walking. Eventually Jack realised that he was not going to get any more reaction from his captain, so he slipped it back into Harold's coat pocket. Harold gave him a playful push and the two of them shook hands. 'You had me going there, Jack.

I really thought I'd had my wallet stolen out there. How did you manage to take it off me without me knowing?'

'Just a little trick I learned at school in South Wales. The boys seemed to enjoy it though, didn't they?'

'Aye I suppose they did, but can you pick on someone else next time you cheeky sod'.

Harold made his way back to his cabin where he removed his linen coat and carefully hung it up. As he sat relaxing on his bed, he looked back on his first ever taste of life in a middle east bazaar. He smiled to himself as he resolved that in future, the only market he would be visiting would be the Monday Market back in Huddersfield.

The next stage of the voyage was one that many of the players had been looking forward to – the passage through the Suez Canal. A modern-day wonder of engineering which had significantly reduced the sailing time to Australia. As the ship made its way into the canal most of the players assembled on deck to observe the local life at close quarters. John Clifford joined the players and spoke to Harold.

'Well did you enjoy your first taste of the middle east Harold?'

'Let's just say it was an experience like nothing I have had the pleasure of previously. Tell the truth John, I was relieved to get back on the ship. Did you go ashore yourself?'

'No Harold, I had the pleasure the last time around, so Mrs Clifford and myself decided not to bother this time.'

'I'm looking forward to this section through the canal though, at least there'll be something to see other than miles and miles of sea.'

'Aye well you'll have plenty of time to do that; it takes

nigh on 15 hours to get through the full length of the canal and to be honest most of the scenery is just desert with an odd palm tree here and there. It will be dark shortly so enjoy it while you can.'

The heat in this section of the journey was intense so after a while observing featureless desert most of the players took shelter inside.

When Harold rose in the morning, he went out on deck and saw that they were still in the canal. His colleague from the Huddersfield team Stanley Moorhouse joined him with a large grin on his face.

'And what's amusing you on this hot sticky morning Stan?'

'Oh I've just bumped into Jack Chilcott and he was telling me about some of the lads last night – have you heard the story?'

'No I haven't Stan, fill me in.'

'Well it seems that a few of the lads had spent quite a while on deck last night staring out into the wilderness and when one of the crew asked them what they were looking at, they said that they were watching out for lions coming down for a drink from the canal, would you believe it?'

Harold started to chuckle 'It sounds like somebody must have missed their geography class, did somebody put them right?'

'Apparently one of the crew – I'm not sure who it was – well they told them they wouldn't see any lions but to keep looking 'cos they have lots of giraffes in this part of Africa and they do come down to the canal at night to drink. They left them there for another half an hour before going back and admitting to them that the only animals they were likely to see would be camels.'

'Ee, they're a gullible lot aren't they. Anyway, I don't know about you Stan but I'm starving, let's go and get some breakfast.'

Eventually the ship finally left the narrow canal and entered the Red Sea where they docked at Port Suez for refuelling. The passengers were not allowed to disembark but a group of acrobats and magicians were allowed on board to entertain the passengers with their tricks.

The temperature continued to rise as they approached the equator where, Mr Clifford pointed out, those players who were crossing the line for the first time would be subjected to King Neptune's court. The ceremony involved being shaved and ducked in a vat of cold water. Given the high temperature on deck the players enjoyed their cooling dip.

Next stop was in Columbo, Ceylon and the players were all keen to go ashore, having been stuck on board for ten days, to stretch their legs on dry land. After a few hours of walking around taking in the sights they were flagging so they decided to use the local form of transport - rickshaws. This soon turned into a racing competition and not surprisingly the lightest member of the squad, Johnny Rogers, was the winner.

Douglas Clark was in mischievous mood and smuggled a harmless snake back onto the boat. After surprising a couple of his team-mates by producing the snake at an opportune moment, Stan Moorhouse came up with a plan to surprise their captain. He gave Douglas Clark a key to the cabin which he shared with Harold Wagstaff and told him to hide the snake in Harold's bed. Stan then sought out his captain and lured him back to the bedroom. However, the joke rebounded on Stan as the snake had been put in the wrong bed. As he sat making conversation with Harold and waited for the snake to appear he did not notice it emerging from his own sheets and climbing onto his trousers and making it's way to his open shirt. When he eventually felt the snake on his bare flesh he panicked and knocked the snake off before running out of the cabin past his laughing team-mates who were listening in just outside the cabin.

Back at sea, as the temperature started to become less oppressive, the players resumed their physical exercises including games of cricket and other deck competitions, interspersed with more strenuous exercises.

Eventually they landed at the Western Australian port of Fremantle before the final leg of the journey on to Sydney via Adelaide.

At last the RMS Otranto pulled into Sydney harbour on 4th June 1914. Joe Houghton was waiting at the dockside to great them, accompanied by a cluster of reporters. John Clifford and his wife led the small group of players down the gang plank where they all received a welcoming handshake from Mr Houghton.

'Welcome to Sydney John, how was the voyage from England?' Joe Houghton asked.

'It's been a good one thank you Joe. The last section has been a bit choppy and a couple of the lads are feeling a bit worse for wear but we're all just pleased to be here at last.'

'Well you've done better than us then. The leg from Colombo was particularly rough and quite a few of the players were really ill'.

The gaggle of reporters were anxious to get some quotes from the new arrivals and were crowding around the players and blocking the way through for the other passengers. Joe Houghton had to shout to be heard above the racket 'They want a quote from you John but it's Harold they really want to speak to.'

John Clifford turned to Harold and grabbed him by the arm 'Come over here Harold with me and we'll say a few words for the reporters and try to make some room for the other passengers to make their way through.'

John Clifford addressed the reporters 'Thank you all gentlemen for your warm welcome here today. It's a pleasure to return to your beautiful city, myself and the players are looking forward to enjoying your hospitality. As you will appreciate we have been in transit now for just over six weeks and are rather tired but tomorrow evening we will be attending a dinner organised by the Lancashire and Yorkshire Societies in our honour where we will be happy to meet you and answer any questions you may have.'

'Just a quick one for Mr Wagstaff' yelled a reporter.

Harold stepped confidently forward 'Go ahead.'

'Do you think this team is as good as the one that Lomas brought here four years ago and went home with the Ashes?'

Another reported joined in and asked 'What are your first opinions of Australia?'

Harold thought for a moment before responding. 'This is my first trip to Australia. What I have seen of the country along the coast has pleased me immensely. There is nothing like seeing places for yourself to get the right idea. As to the team, all I can say is, we mean to do our best and win as many matches as we can. I don't think there Is anything more than that to be said' came Harold's diplomatic reply.

Joe Houghton raised both hands 'Thank you all gentlemen, now if you would excuse us, we'd like to get on our way to the hotel.'

As they made their way to the hotel by horse drawn carriage Joe explained the plans for their first day. 'When you arrive at the hotel the other lads will be waiting to welcome you, then you'll have a couple of hours to settle in and unpack. This afternoon we have a light training session planned which I think you'll want to join in, remember we have our first game on Saturday. I don't think any of you lads will be ready for that will you?'

A chorus of 'I'm ready boss' went up from the players.

Joe Houghton smiled 'I might have guessed that I would get that response, we'll see how you all go in training this afternoon and then the selection committee will decide on the team this evening.' He turned his attention to Harold 'The local police have asked if you, as the tour captain, would be available to referee a game for them this afternoon. How do you feel about that?'

'Truth be told Mr Houghton I would rather have a run out with the lads, but we don't want to let the local bobbies down do we, got to stay on the right side of the local police.'

CHAPTER 13 –
EARLY SETBACKS
FOR THE
NORTHERN UNION

Thursday 4th June, Sydney

That evening the two managers along with Wagstaff, the captain and Willie Davies the vice-captain sat down to select the team for the touring party's first game. The opposition would be Metropolis, a selection of the best players in Sydney.

Joe Houghton pointed out the calibre of the opposition 'It'll be pretty much the test team, I'm afraid. The Sydney clubs provide the majority of the players for the New South Wales and Australian team.'

'Aye Mr Clifford said as much to me on the ship coming over' replied Harold. 'Will my old mate Snowy Deane be playing?'

'Aye lad, they've appointed him as the captain. Had a few tussles with him have you then?' Joe Houghton replied.

'You can say that again Joe. Damn good player, and a grand bloke too. Rozzy introduced me to him when we were laking at Oldham a year or two back. Rozzy toured with him you know, the first time they came over. It was that year we had the awful winter and the mills were all on strike.'

'Well you might be crossing swords with our Mr Deane next season Harold, rumour is he's on his way to Hull' came the response from Joe Houghton.

'Well I never' Willie Davies chimed in 'but I thought they'd introduced a residence qualification rule now, before an Aussie could sign for a Northern Union club.'

'Ah, well this is where it gets interesting' Joe Houghton looked around to check that he had their undivided attention. 'It seems that Oldham retained his registration when Sid returned to Australia two or three years back, so they will get a transfer fee from Hull and the lad won't need to spend a year or two kicking his heels whilst he qualifies.'

'Is it a done deal then Mr Houghton?' Harold enquired.

'No Harold, not as I understand it, I believe they have to get clearance from the Northern Union. So, watch this space as they say.'

'Well at least they won't have Messenger in their team this time. What a player he was' added John Clifford, 'he could change a game in the twinkle of an eye.'

'Actually, there is a Messenger in the team, it's his younger brother Wally, he's another goal kicker an all' Joe Houghton added.

'Alright gentlemen' Joe Houghton brought them back to the matter in hand. We have established that this is going to be a really tough match, so we need to field as strong a team as possible.'

'I've not seen any of the lads in action, so I'll take a back seat on this one' suggested Harold.

'Are we all agreed that we should only select those players who were in the first group to arrive?' the proposal came from John Clifford.

Willie Davies raised the forefinger of his right hand 'If I might make a suggestion on that?' He looked around and got the nod to continue. 'I thought Johnny Rogers looked very sharp at training this afternoon and he was in blistering form at the end of last season if I recall correctly.'

The full squad chosen to represent the Northern Union on the tour of 1914. (Courtesy Mike Baxter).

Harold nodded 'Aye true enough Willie, and he has been working hard, as we all have, on the trip over. But we've only just got off the ship and two days to recover is not a lot is it?'

'What does the lad think about laking on Saturday, has anyone asked him?' John Clifford again.

Willie responded 'I had a few words with him after training and the lads as keen as mustard to have a run out.'

The conversation continued and eventually the thirteen names for Saturday were unanimously agreed. Rogers was selected at scrum half on the proviso that his fitness would be re-assessed on the morning of the match.

As the small group relaxed after agreeing the team for Saturday John Clifford asked Joe Houghton what sort of attendance they were expecting at the weekend.

'Apparently we could be in for a record attendance' came the reply, 'probably 40,000 maybe more.'

'Really? So many?' the visibly shocked Harold asked.

'It seems that Rugby League, as the locals here refer to it, is really taking off in New South Wales: more so than in Queensland and New Zealand. In Sydney itself they go mad for it. I was speaking to an Aussie friend who I met on the last tour and he says the interest in the tour is sky high. All the newspapers – throughout Australia not just in Sydney – have been publishing regular articles about the tour. Every time a few more players were selected it was in all the papers.' At this point he turned to address Harold 'Let me warn you, young man, they are particularly fascinated by you. You come with quite a reputation. They're amazed at a 22-year-old actually captaining the touring team, they're even referring to you as a prodigy.'

Harold looked embarrassed 'It looks like I've got a lot to live up to then. I just hope that I don't let the other lads down.'

'There's no chance of that Harold' John Clifford re-assured him as he patted him on the back.

Joe Houghton continued 'The press follow us everywhere, they seem to have an insatiable appetite for quotes and interviews. It'll be nice to be able to share the workload with the two of you for a change. But seriously Harold, they are hungry for information about you. They keep asking me if I think you are better than Lomas and

Messenger – Dally not Wally. I guarantee they will ask you the same questions – so, be prepared.'

'Thanks for the advice Mr Houghton I'll make sure that I'm ready when the questions come.'

John Clifford then cheekily asked 'Just as a matter of interest Joe, what answer did you give when they asked you to compare our skipper with the other two?'

'I simply told them that Harold here is a completely different kettle of fish to the other two. They had attributes which Harold does not possess but he more than makes up for them with his other talents. I actually told them that comparisons are odious.' He paused for a moment 'But I did tell them that once they saw Harold play, they would not be disappointed.'

'Thanks again, Mr Houghton. I hope I can live up to the billing you've given me. Now if you gentlemen will excuse me, it's been a long and exciting day, so I think I'll make my way to bed.'

Harold and Willie Davies said their good nights and left the two managers to bring each other up to speed on what had been happening since the last time they were together and to plan how to handle the next few days.

Friday 5th June, Sydney

The training session on the day before a match was usually a light work out and a last chance to work on some combinations. On the way to the training pitch Harold had a private word with Johnny Rogers 'How are you feeling today Johnny, did you get a good night's sleep?'

'As a matter of fact' Johnny started in his strong welsh accent, 'now you come to mention it 'Arold, I had a lovely night's sleep. Slept like a baby I did. I'm really looking forward to getting a run out on the grass today.'

Harold looked around to make sure they were out of

earshot of the other players 'Well don't overdo it Johnny, try to conserve your energy, don't go mad.'

'Why do you say that Harold, I'm bursting with energy. I'm telling you I can't wait to get my hands on the ball, and you expect me to take it easy?'

Johnny Rogers seen here in his Welsh strip, made his tour debut just two days after arriving in Sydney following a six week journey. (Courtesy Huddersfield RL Heritage).

Harold didn't speak but as he looked at Johnny, he raised his eyebrows.

'It took a few seconds for Johnny Rogers to get the message, then his eyes lit up. 'No! Are you telling me I'm in the team tomorrow?' There was a pause 'Harold am I really in the team?'

'I'm sworn to secrecy Johnny, Mr Houghton will be announcing the team after training. But if I was you, I wouldn't over do it, and that's all I can say.' Johnny Rogers had a spring in his step as the pair of them entered the changing rooms.

The touring party had hired a local trainer, David Murray, to put the lads through their paces. Harold observed with interest as the players who had been in Australia for over week went through some combinations. He was not overly impressed with what he saw but decided to keep his own council for the time being.

After training, the whole touring party assembled in the hotel lobby where Joe Houghton read out the team for Saturday's game. As each player's name was announced there was a round of applause.

Houghton began 'At fullback we have Alf Wood, right wing will be Jack Robinson, with Bert Jenkins at centre. Willie Davies, who will captain the team will be at left centre with Frank Williams on the wing. Johnny Rogers and Stuart Prosser will play at half back. In the forwards we have James Clampitt, Rattler Roman and Billy Jarman, who will make up the front row. Dave Holland and John Smailes will be in the second row and Joe Guerin will be the lock.'

The players who hadn't been selected, although disappointed, were quick to congratulate their team-mates and wish them luck for the game.

The team enjoyed a warm welcome from the combined Lancashire and Yorkshire Societies at the reception in their honour on the Friday evening. The players selected for the first match were sensibly restrained in their consumption as they looked forward, somewhat nervously, to the first big match of the tour.

Saturday 6th June, Sydney

On the morning of the match the atmosphere in Sydney was electric. People were flocking in from the suburbs all morning and making their way to the Sydney Cricket Ground. By the time the gates were opened at 11 o'clock a large crowd were waiting outside, keen to get the best position for the greatly anticipated meeting between their local heroes and the British Lions.

A big crowd had been anticipated and those expectations were fully justified as the crowd grew and grew. When the players entered the field both teams received a fantastic reception from the crowd which was estimated at over 45,000.

As Joe Houghton took his seat in the stand he was

flanked by John Clifford and Harold Wagstaff with the other tourists in the row behind them. 'They said they were expecting a big crowd today gentlemen, but I can't believe just how many spectators have actually turned up.'

'It's quite a sight isn't it. It looks like half the population of Sydney is here' replied John Clifford. 'Let's hope the game is a suitable spectacle for them all.'

'I don't know who the selectors for the Metropolis side are, but they've certainly chosen a very strong team' added Harold. 'Besides my old mate Snowy Deane, they've Harold Horder, Wally Messenger and 'Pony' Halloway in the backs. The forwards look good too, there's Sandy Pearce and Frank Burge who are both top notch players. It's going to be a tough ask for the lads in their first real match of the tour.'

'Well Harold we shall soon see if the lads are ready for the battle won't we' came the response from John Clifford.

In the event it did not take long to see just how good and committed the Metropolis players actually were, as they simply dominated the tourists. After the home team had opened the scoring with a couple of penalties to lead 4 to nil the tourists suffered their first injury of the tour when Alf Wood required attention for an ankle injury. After a long delay Wood had to leave the field, the tourist moved Billy Jarman to fullback. Shortly afterwards Hallett landed a fine drop goal for the home side to stretch their lead to six points.

Wood was able to return to the fray but was injured again as the home team registered their first try through a brilliant move by Harry Horder which Wally Messenger converted. The home team now had a lead of eleven points and the tourists were reduced to twelve men. John Clifford turned to Harold 'It's not looking good for the boys is it Harold.'

'I just hope that Alf isn't too badly injured. I'll go down to the changing rooms at half time and see how he is.'

Joe Houghton looked frustrated as he clenched his fist and beat his knee in frustration 'I really wish the Northern Union committee would see sense on this substitute rule. We're down to twelve men and if the other side get an injury, they'll just bring on their reserve, it's crazy.'

Things did improve slightly for the tourists as Joe Guerin, standing in as goal kicker in place of the absent Wood, landed a fine penalty from near the touchline. That was as good as it got in the first half as the Metropolis ran in two further tries from Norman and Halloway, both converted by Messenger who also landed a penalty. At half time the score stood at 23 points to 2 in favour of the home team.

The second half continued in similar fashion to the first as the home team added further tries from Kelly, Deane and a second for Horder. All three were converted by Messenger to make the score 38 points to 2. To their credit the tiring British team rallied and scored consolation tries through Holland and Prosser. Guerin missed an easy conversion so Rogers took over kicking duties for the final try, and his conversion attempt went in off the post. The final score was an embarrassing 38 points to 10 victory for the Metropolis.

The majority of spectators left the ground a little disappointed at the one-sided nature of the game but delighted that their local heroes had put in such a fine attacking performance.

The dressing room of the beaten tourists was full of

tired and dejected players and an air of gloom hung over the room. As Harold Wagstaff and the two managers walked into the room the players were quiet. Harold was the first to break the silence. 'Come on boys cheer up, it was only the first match; they were just too strong for us today and too sharp. As the tour progresses, I'm confident that we'll improve.'

Bert Jenkins chimed in 'He's right boys, the last time I was over here with Jimmy Lomas we lost to this lot in the first game, and the one after actually. But look how that turned out, we still came back with the ashes didn't we.'

'It didn't help losing Alfie in the first half either' added Willie Davies. He looked around to see Alf Wood but he had already got changed and left. 'Does anyone know how bad the injury is?'

Harold responded 'Fortunately it's doesn't look too serious, just a sprain, hopefully he'll be back in a couple of weeks. The other good news is we don't have to wait long to have a chance to show the Aussies what we are really made of. We play New South Wales on Monday and my guess is they will probably select the same team, so, after the way they played today, they will be very confident.'

'Harold is right lads' John Clifford added 'there's no time for feeling sorry for ourselves on this tour. We'll have a light training session in the morning. Check who's fit to play and then pick the team for Monday. By the way lads, the attendance today was over 50,000 and they are expecting another big crowd on Monday.'

Back at the team's hotel the two managers invited Harold and Willie Davies to join them for a chat. John Clifford opened the discussion. 'I just thought it would be a good idea to share our thoughts after today's performance. Willie, how did it feel to you out there on the pitch.'

Willie rubbed his chin with his right hand and shifted uneasily in his chair. 'To tell you the truth gents it was bloody hard work. It was very hot out there and the pitch was rock hard. Losing Alfie was a setback, but they were already on top before he was injured, so we can't use that as an excuse. They dominated our forwards and seemed to win so much ball at the scrum.'

'Thanks for that Willie.' John Clifford turned to Harold 'What did you make of it Harold from up in the stand?'

'Well, for a start I thought all the lads put a massive effort in, so no criticism on that score. Willie is right though we lost the forward battle, and they starved us of possession. When we did have the ball our combinations just weren't good enough to cause them problems, apart from the last few minutes when I think they had relaxed a bit.'

'Joe what are your thoughts?' John Clifford turned his attention to his co-manager.

'I think these two have summed it up to a tee John. Forwards beaten, not enough possession and poor use of it when we got it. The question is what can we do about it in the time that's available?'

'We can make changes to the team for a start' responded John Clifford. 'Harold do you think our Huddersfield lads will be ready for Monday?'

'We're all champing at the bit Mr Clifford truth be told. But whether we'd do any better than the lads who played today remains to be seen.'

After further discussion it was agreed that at Sunday's training session Harold would take charge of the backs and focus on their combinations whilst the forwards would work on their scrummaging techniques.

Monday 8th June, Sydney

As the players woke on the morning of the second match and peered out of the hotel window, they had a pleasant surprise. It was overcast and wet, conditions with which they were much more familiar.

The Northern Union had been asked to announce their team on Saturday evening but the team which actually took the field showed a further two changes from the original selection. The two wingers from the first match, Robinson and Williams had originally been retained, however on the morning of the match they were still feeling the effects of the previous game, so they were replaced in the team by Willie Davies and Stan Moorhouse. Harold Wagstaff's prediction regarding the opposition proved correct and the New South Wales selectors opted to keep the same team that had walloped the tourists two days earlier. Not surprisingly the Northern Union side didn't. Willie Davies, Bert Jenkins, Johnny Rogers, Billy Jarman and Dave Holland were the only survivors from Saturday's beaten team. Gwyn Thomas came in for the injured Alf Wood at full back and Wagstaff, Stan Moorhouse and Billy Hall were selected in the backs. Percy Coldrick, Douglas Clark, Chick Johnson and Jack Chilcott came in to strengthen the forward pack. The team, therefore, comprised of five players from the Huddersfield club, three from Wigan, two each from Leeds and Oldham and one from Widnes.

As the morning wore on it became apparent that neither the poor weather nor the poor performance by the tourists in the first game was going to have a significant effect on the attendance. Sydney was once more awash with fans making their way back to the Sydney Cricket

Ground for the second big match of the tour.

In conditions more suited to the tourists the game was a much closer affair. The tourists pack was lighter and more mobile than the one selected for the previous game and they were able to claim their share of the ball from the scrums. The backs, whilst playing with greater fluency than previously, were still not as cohesive as the opposition. The work put in on the training ground had resulted in improvements but not enough to topple their confident opponents.

The Northern Union took the lead through a fine try by Wagstaff, but their lead was pegged back shortly afterwards when Messenger landed a penalty. He was injured shortly afterwards, and his place was taken by Fraser. This was the first time that the tourists had experienced the Australian replacement rule, but it would not be the last. Another penalty, this time from Horder gave the home team a one-point lead. It was a tight game and the crowd were enthralled as play went from end to end. The tourists were very much in the game at this stage until the injury curse struck again. On this occasion Hall was the unfortunate player as he had to leave the field after only 25 minutes suffering from a head injury.

At half time New South Wales led by 6 points to 3, courtesy of another penalty from Horder.

The second half continued in the same end to end fashion and, despite being a man down, the tourists were giving as good as they got. Both sides attacked with great intent, but the defences stood firm. Eventually Horder landed another penalty and in the closing minutes Kelly crossed for the home team's solitary try. The game ended in an 11 points to 3 win for New South Wales in what had been a thrilling contest. The large crowd of 48,660 spectators had been richly entertained by an exciting game in which the tourists had performed much better, having shown a few flashes of the brilliance that had been expected from them.

The newspapers had, justifiably, been very critical of the tourist's performance in the first game and the criticism after this second consecutive defeat continued, albeit at a less extreme level.

That evening the tourists were entertained for dinner by the New South Wales Rugby League. After dinner the Chairman of the New South Wales Rugby League raised a toast to the King, and his deputy raised one to the Northern Union touring team. John Clifford responded for the visiting team by saying 'Five out of thirteen men on the field today only got off the ship on Thursday; and it must necessarily be some weeks before the men are really in their best form. When we return to England I hope that we will be able to say that this team was superior to that of 1910, and so satisfy all the home critics.'

This was followed by a few words from Harold Wagstaff, who, in his capacity as captain of the touring team, said 'We will win like men, and lose like gentlemen and when we return from Queensland I think we will win.' Finally, Willie Davies, the vice-captain proposed a toast to the New South Wales team and added 'the New South Wales team had played the better games, and he too hoped the Northern Union team would show better form when they returned from Brisbane.'

Harold in his speech also made reference to the fact that the tourists had, in both games, been a man short for a large proportion of both matches. He expressed his hope that in future, touring teams would adopt the principle of 'when in Rome do as the Romans', a direct reference to the controversial substitute rule.

Despite the two early setbacks there was still an air of confidence in the tourist's camp that the players in the squad would improve as they benefitted from more time together to work on their fitness and their combinations.

Back at the hotel the all the players went straight to bed; but the two managers and their captain did not follow them. They had much to discuss. Two defeats in their first two matches was a bitter pill to swallow.

Harold started the ball rolling. 'In the first game we were starved of possession and were loose with our combinations. In the second game Percy Coldrick and the other forwards gave us an equal share of the ball but our combinations still weren't good enough.'

'I think you may be being a bit harsh there Harold' John Clifford responded. 'I saw a real improvement in our link up play in the second game, and we had several good, sweeping moves which looked promising.'

'Yes, that's true John, they did look promising. That's the whole point though isn't it. With the exception of the try we scored, we didn't turn any of those promising movements into points, did we?'

'Well, that's true enough' conceded John Clifford.

'I reckon we need to spend all the time we have available for practice, working on those combinations. By all accounts the teams up in Queensland are not as strong as the ones down here in Sydney, so we should have the chance to polish our link up play in real match conditions.'

'Harold is right John' added Joe Houghton. 'When we lost the first two games in 1910 that's exactly what we did isn't it. The lads worked harder in training and eventually it started to pay dividends.'

John Clifford added 'We don't have a lot of time though do we? We've got a game against Queensland on Saturday, then we've got Ipswich on Wednesday and then we're back in Brisbane for the first test match the following Saturday. Queensland will be no pushover either, they've got some decent players. I've heard good reports about the Bolewski brothers who are all pushing for places in the full Australian side.'

'Point taken John. Look we've got a full day tomorrow and we can train on Wednesday morning before we set off for Brisbane on Wednesday evening. Thursday we are in transit all day that just leaves Friday. I suggest morning and afternoon sessions tomorrow and Friday as well as one on Wednesday.' Harold was keen to get started.

'How do you think the lads will respond to that Harold?' John Clifford asked.

'They're all proud lads' responded Harold. 'These two defeats have hurt every one of us. Every single one of those lads is desperate to put those defeats behind us and get back to winning. There won't be any opposition from them, I'll guarantee it.'

Joe Houghton interjected 'I hate to put a damper on your enthusiasm gentlemen, but there won't be any training on Friday morning as the Queensland Rugby League have arranged a reception in our honour at the Carlton Club for Friday morning.'

'Damn and blast I'd forgotten all about that' strong language indeed from the captain. 'I suppose we'll just have to work that bit harder on the sessions we can run won't we.'

'That's the spirit Harold' joked Joe Houghton, as he gave the young man an encouraging pat on the back.

'Anyway' Harold stood up, 'I'm off to bed, we've got a busy day ahead of us tomorrow.'

The two managers wished him good night. Joe Houghton turned to John Clifford 'Time for a nightcap John?'

'Why not Joe, I think we've earned it.'

Tuesday 9th June, Sydney

The world famous Sydney Cricket Ground, known throughout the sporting world as the SCG. Scene of the first two matches of the tour as well as the last two test matches. (Source Wikipedia).

Tuesday's papers were predictably critical of the touring squad and, in particular, their policy of not replacing injured players. Blame for this was, incorrectly, placed on the shoulders of the team managers even though they had lobbied the Northern Union to allow them to replace injured players in the same way that the home side did.

In fact, the majority of the papers were already writing off the touring team's chances of regaining the Ashes. However, the correspondent for the Sydney Sun was an exception to the rule. In his article on the 7th June he expressed some sympathy for the tourists, pointing out that it was unfair to expect players who had recently spent six weeks onboard ship to be matched up against such strong opposition in their first two games. He argued that it was too early to write off the tourists as their form would undoubtedly improve as they acclimatised to local conditions. Wise words indeed.

Wednesday 10th June, Sydney Harbour

After two strenuous training sessions on Tuesday and one on Wednesday morning the tourists were on their travels again as they made the train journey north to Brisbane, where the next game of the tour would take place. John Clifford's suggestion that they would travel by ship turned out to be incorrect as they decided to travel overland by train. The journey was an experience in more ways than one. The first part of the journey was not too bad, with a stop off at Newcastle where they had to rush a five-course meal down in a few minutes. What didn't get eaten was carried onto the train to be finished. The train was a night sleeper, but no-one got a full night's sleep as the train ran over a stray cow and it took two hours to remove the dead animal from underneath the engine.

The team had to change trains at Walla Garra near the border with Queensland onto a narrow gauge line with smaller carriages which wobbled alarmingly at every bend of the journey. They eventually arrived in Brisbane late on Thursday night.

During the first part of the journey Harold and the two managers sat together to review the previous day's training.

'Well Harold' John Clifford began 'How do you think the training sessions went?'

'We're making progress John, no doubt about that, but there's still a lot of room for improvement. With a few more training sessions and a couple of games we should be peaking in time for the test series. When you come to think of it, it's really not that surprising is it? We've got the Northern Union's best players here, no doubt about it, but we all come from different clubs who all have their own systems and styles of play. It stands to reason that it will take some time to perfect our linkup play and combinations and get to know each other's strengths and weaknesses.'

As the weary travellers finally arrived at their hotel in Brisbane and headed straight to bed, Joe Houghton turned to John Clifford and observed 'It's just as well we are being entertained in the morning John, after that tortuous journey I don't think any of the lads would be up for one of Harold's stiff training sessions in the morning.'

Saturday 13th June, Brisbane

Harold's prediction was correct and all the players, excluding the injured ones, had put maximum effort into all the training sessions. There was a renewed air of confidence in the camp and Harold could sense that the adversity and criticism they were all facing had helped to draw them closer together and a real team spirit was developing amongst the players.

The Northern Union team included the five players who had not yet made an appearance on tour so far. Alf Francis, Fred Smith and Jack O'Garra were selected in the backs and Fred Longstaff and Dick Ramsdale played in the forwards.

The Queensland team had also been very thorough in their preparations and had held several practice sessions together. The local press noted that never before had a Queensland team been as thorough in their preparation as this one. As expected, all three of the Bolewski brothers were selected, Mick was appointed captain and played at full back whilst Henry and Walter appeared in the centres.

The attendance of 12,000 was considerably less than

the Sydney games had attracted but was still a record for rugby league in Queensland. The crowd were well entertained by an open and fast game in which the tourists took a 13 points to nil lead at the interval. Frank Williams on the wing benefitted from some improved link up play and scored a couple of tries and Alf Francis on the other wing added another. In the second half a further try from Francis extended the lead before the home team hit back with two tries of their own and at one point they had pulled the lead back to six points. A penalty goal late on secured an 18 points to 10 win for the touring side.

For the third game in a row the Northern Union had finished with only twelve men. On this occasion it was not injury which caused this but the sending-off of John Smales. No one in the press box could work out what his misdemeanour had been but when questioned after the match the referee indicated that he had been guilty of 'unsportsmanlike behaviour'. It later transpired that the offence that John Smales had committed was jumping over an opponent that went to tackle him rather than running into the tackler. A strange decision indeed as this was not even considered an offence in either England or New South Wales.

The record crowd went home well satisfied having been treat to a feast of fast open rugby by both teams and although their team had been defeated, they had put up a fine performance. Most agreed that the Northern Union fully deserved their victory. And so, after their victory in Brisbane the tourists were in a positive frame of mind as they looked forward to their trip to Ipswich on the following Wednesday. Their captain though was not satisfied.

At their regular post-match review in the hotel lobby he

made his feelings known. 'I just don't think we are performing at our best possible level yet. We are still having periods when we switch off.'

'You really are a hard man to please aren't you Harold' Joe Houghton chided him in a good-natured tone.

'I suppose you could say that Joe. But just look at how we let them back into the game in the second half. At 16 nil up we should have put the match to bed, instead we ended up hanging on until we got that last penalty. If we do that next week in the test match the Aussies will make us pay dearly.'

'You've got a point there Harold but what can we do to stop those lapses in concentration?' John Clifford took over the questioning.

'I think we need to step up on the fitness John. Concentration tends to slip when you're tired. I reckon we need to do a bit more work on our fitness before the first test match next week.'

'Well at least the combinations are much better now. I think we've got that sorted, don't you?' Joe Houghton was directing his comments to Harold.

Harold shook his head 'There's still room for improvement there as well Joe. Yes, we scored some good tries from well constructed moves, but with the players we have at our disposal we should be doing even better.'

'So, a bit more work to do there as well then Harold?'

'Aye, we'll be working on that this week rest assured' came the reply from Harold.

John Clifford leaned forward 'Ipswich won't be a pushover by any means, but with the first test coming up next Saturday I think we should rest a few of the lads don't you?'

Joe Houghton was the first to respond 'Yes I agree with

that John. With Alfie Wood being injured we should rest Gwyn Thomas, he's the only specialist full back we have who's fit.'

'Who are we going to pick at full back against Ipswich though, if we don't pick Gwyn and Alfie isn't fit?' asked John Clifford.

'Billie Jarman would get my vote; he's done the job a few times for Leeds hasn't he?' suggested Harold.

'That's a good idea Harold. He's a handy lad to have around, isn't he?' agreed Joe Houghton.

'OK, that's full back sorted, just another twelve to go' joked John Clifford.

The three of them worked their way through the team. The managers suggested that Harold should sit this one out, but he was having none of that.

'Sorry gentlemen but I really need to be out there on the field to call the moves. The extra game will benefit me as well, I don't think I've reached my peak of fitness yet.'

The officials of the Queensland Rugby League had a lot to be pleased about that evening. A record-breaking crowd had been enthralled by a great game of flowing rugby and their team had put up a brave show. In one week's time they would be hosting a full international match as the Northern Union were due to face the might of Australia in the first Ashes test, also in Brisbane – or so they thought!

That evening they received a telegram from the New South Wales Rugby League which would wipe the smiles off their faces and have severe ramifications for the test series and indeed the rest of the tour.

In the cable the New South Wales Rugby League informed the Queensland Rugby League that none of the Sydney based players would be travelling to Brisbane for the game. A team representing Australia without their best players – as the Sydney contingent would surely be – was unthinkable. The Queensland Rugby League were determined not to take this setback lying down and over the next few days there were frequent communications between the representatives of the two bodies in which the Queensland Rugby League tried to persuade the New South Wales Rugby League to change their minds. The Queensland Rugby League decided not to publicise the actions of the New South Wales Rugby League in the vain belief that they may still be able to bring about a change of heart. By the time it got to Thursday, just two days before the game, it was obvious that the Sydney players were not coming and the Queensland Rugby League had no option but to go public and downgrade the game to a repeat of the previous week's game, a Queensland select versus the Northern Union.

The Northern Union had been preparing all week for a test match only to find that it would not take place. Not surprisingly when the news became public there was an outcry. The Queensland Rugby League laid the responsibility for the change in status of the game firmly at the door of the New South Wales Rugby League and exonerated the Northern Union from any responsibility. Joe Houghton and John Clifford were also upset as the first test had now been put back a week to the 27th June. The second test was already scheduled for two days later and the third and final test was on the following Saturday. Three test matches in eight days was a tall order indeed. In addition to the three tests the tourists also had a game against Bathhurst on the middle Thursday.

The following letter from Mr H Sutherland, Honorary Secretary of the Queensland Rugby League, appeared in the Brisbane Daily Standard on Friday 19th June:

'When the programme of the tour of the Northern Union football team was drawn the fixture for June 20th was set down as Australia v England to be played at Brisbane. This advice was sent to the Queensland Rugby League before the English players arrived in Australia, and, acting upon it the Queensland League let it be generally known that the Englishmen's second match in Brisbane would be between Australia and England, and advertised the match as such.

However, on Saturday night at about eight o'clock an urgent telegram was received from the New South Wales Rugby League informing the Queensland body that no New South Wales players would be available for next Saturday's match. The local league did not let the matter rest at that and, in the last few days we have been in constant telegraphic communication with the Sydney officials in an endeavour to have the fixture played as advertised. The Southern league, however, would not alter its decision and the Queensland League has no other alternative but to play a Queensland team against the Englishmen tomorrow.

It was through no fault of the Queensland League that the test match has had to be abandoned, nor are the Englishmen in any way to blame. The reason why the matter was not made public earlier was that the local governing body thought that they might possibly be able to arrange with New South Wales to send players, but the latest advice received yesterday afternoon was to the effect that no Southern players were available, and that the decision already conveyed to Queensland must stand. The fault, therefore, lies solely at the door of the New South Wales League.'

The Northern Union Managers, Joe Houghton and John Clifford wisely stayed out of the argument between the rival bodies until after the match with Queensland had been played. A few days later, when the dust had settled, Joe Houghton was quoted in the press, 'Yes, it is right to say we are not satisfied, but we waived our claims rather than cause friction. It was suggested we cancel our Bathurst visit but this we declined to do. We had no intention of penalising Bathurst people on account of an irregularity to which they were not party. We shall carry out our tour, whatever happens, in every detail.'

Wednesday 17th June, Ipswich

The team selected for the match at Ipswich may not have been the best line-up from the touring squad, but it was far too strong for the local side. The final score of 45 points to 8 in the tourist's favour was a fair reflection of the dominant performance provided by them. Alf Francis continued his try scoring form with five tries, making it seven from his two appearances.

For once Harold expressed satisfaction with the team's performance, but still offered a note of caution to temper his optimism.

'Well then' started John Clifford 'will that do for you?'

'A lot better John. I really think we're beginning to click. Let's not get carried away though the opposition on Saturday will be a much tougher proposition. But if we carry on doing the right things consistently as we did today, we'll put ourselves in with a great chance in the test match. It's going to be difficult to pick the team for Saturday the way some of these lads have played today.'

John Clifford continued 'There'll be another training session tomorrow when we'll see who's fit and ready to play and then we'll pick the team in the evening.'

'Have they announced the Australian team yet?' enquired Harold.

'I've not heard anything yet, came the response from

John Clifford. 'How about you Joe have you heard anything?'

'No, I haven't and there is a rumour going around, that there's a problem with the Sydney based players.' Joe Houghton paused for thought for a moment before continuing. 'I would have expected the lads from Sydney to be already on their way and be here by tomorrow at the latest, it's really very strange.'

Harold was clearly taken aback 'You're not suggesting that the Sydney lads might not come, are you? They'll be making up the majority of the Australian team, won't they?'

'Let's not jump to conclusions here, we've had no word from the Queensland officials, so we go ahead and plan for the test match.' As ever John Clifford was the voice of reason. 'We'll know soon enough; in the meantime, we prepare for a Test match. Not a word to the rest of the lads Harold, we don't want them to lose focus at such a critical time.'

Harold said good night and left the managers in the lounge. As he made his way to bed, he reflected on the conversation which had just taken place. The team had been building up for this match and so had he. The first test was what he had been focussing on since they landed. He knew how important it would be to win that first game of the series if they were going to achieve their objective and bring back the Ashes to Great Britain. And yet... as he ran it over in his mind, another week would give the team more time to improve their fitness and practice their inter-play and teamwork. He resolved to put it to the back of his mind and make the best of whatever transpired. As John Clifford had pointed out they would know for sure soon enough, given the time it took to travel from Sydney to Brisbane.

Thursday 18th June, Sydney

When Harold joined the rest of his team-mates at breakfast there was a real buzz of excitement in the camp. After a convincing win the previous day and with the prospect of the imminent test match, everyone was wondering who would be chosen for the big match. Harold kept his thoughts to himself as he considered the conversation of the previous evening. 'Now let's keep our feet on the ground lads, that was a good performance yesterday, but we need to keep working hard at our game if we are going to beat the Aussies.'

'Of course we're going to beat the Aussies' chirped Gwyn Thomas 'we're the pride of the Northern Union.'

The statement was followed by a cheer from the rest of the team.

At that point they were joined by Joe Houghton and the lads all settled down again.

There is nothing to compare with winning to build a team's confidence, Harold thought to himself. Just over a week ago the lads were down having been convincingly beaten by the pride of Sydney. Two wins later and the confidence was back. But confidence can soon become cockiness and complacency and Harold was determined to make sure that that would not happen with this team. When all the players had settled down for breakfast he announced 'Mr Houghton and Mr Clifford will be watching you all very carefully at training today; and the team for Saturday's test match will be selected this evening based on how you all perform. So, let's all concentrate on our own performance and then we'll take on the Aussies on Saturday.'

All the players settled down and had their breakfasts in

relative silence as they considered what Harold had said. Harold carefully looked around and saw the look of determination in all the players faces that he wanted to see. Once the lads who had played the day before had run off their stiffness the team got down to some serious work at the training session. Every single one of the fit players was desperate to be a part of the test team and gave their best efforts throughout the training session. Harold took a moment out to chat with the two managers. 'Any word from Sydney gents?' he asked.

'Not a dicky bird I'm afraid' responded Joe Houghton. 'And nothing from the Queensland Rugby League either. I'll speak to them this afternoon and see if I can find out what is going on. I've got a funny feeling that there won't be a test match this weekend though.'

'The lads are really going for it today Harold' added John Clifford. 'Those well-chosen words of yours at breakfast seem to have done the trick.'

'We're getting there John, but you know' he paused 'another week before the first test match wouldn't be such a bad thing. A couple more matches and more good work on the training pitch wouldn't do us any harm at all.'

'I take your point Harold, but the decision is out of our hands isn't it. We just have to prepare for a test match and if it is delayed so be it.'

After the training session had finished Joe Houghton made arrangements to meet his opposite number at the Queensland Rugby League, Mr H Sunderland, later that day.

Joe Houghton received a warm welcome and vigorous handshake from Queensland Rugby League's secretary. 'I hope that you are enjoying your visit to Queensland Mr Houghton.'

'Thank you, Mr Sunderland' Joe Houghton replied. 'May I say how welcoming the people of Queensland have been to us all, and how much we are enjoying our stay here in Brisbane.'

'I'm pleased to hear that Mr Houghton. However, I will not beat around the bush, I think I know why you are here, and I am afraid that I have some rather bad news to share with you today. The New South Wales Rugby League have placed us in the invidious position of having to downgrade the match on Saturday. Instead of the expected test match against the full Australian Rugby League side you will be meeting a Queensland select thirteen.'

'I won't say that this is a complete surprise as we have heard a few rumours circulating to that effect. Naturally we are disappointed to have the rumours confirmed. But tell me Mr Sunderland what are the circumstances which have created this situation.'

'The facts, Mr Houghton, are as follows. Last Saturday, the 13th June, we received a telegram from Sydney informing us that the New South Wales players would not be travelling to Brisbane for the game. No explanation was given to us. We earnestly believed that, as we were in the right on this matter, we would be able to persuade them to have a change of heart. For this reason, we decided not to go public on the matter. In the meantime, we have been in communication with our New South Wales counterparts in an attempt to reverse the decision, but to no avail. Today we have received formal confirmation that the players from Sydney will not be travelling North for the game. I have already prepared a statement for the press to make everyone aware of the change and the circumstances which have led to it. I have a copy of the statement here.' He passed a typed document to Joe Houghton.

Houghton read the statement carefully and then handed it back to Mr Sutherland. 'I'm pleased to see that you have not attached any blame to ourselves and let me assure you that we have not been party to this change. I think I know why the New South Wales Rugby League have made this change but please be assured that there was no pressure from our side to do this. With the wonderful attendances at all our games the financial success of our tour is already guaranteed. Indeed we see ourselves as ambassadors for the game and are keen to play in as many places as possible to foster the development of the game in the wider area of Australia and not just focus on Sydney where the game is already well established.'

'I am pleased to hear that Mr Houghton. I know that the people of Brisbane will be disappointed that a full test match is not taking place, but I am sure they will turn out in good numbers and give your team a great reception on Saturday.'

'Now, if you will excuse me Mr Sunderland I will get back to the hotel and pass the news on to the Team Manager, Mr Clifford, and the rest of the touring party. I know that they will be disappointed but, rest assured, we will be assembling a strong team to meet your selection on Saturday.'

The two administrators shook hands and Joe Houghton left to go back to the hotel to pass the news on.

Joe Houghton had a brief chat with John Clifford and they decided to call a meeting of the full squad to give them the news. Not surprisingly there was a general air of disappointment within the group when they heard the news.

Harold got to his feet 'Right lads, we're all disappointed that the test match is off this week. But that means we have at least two more games in which we can work to improve our performances. It's up to us to make the best of the opportunity and make sure that when we do meet the full Australian side, we are in tip top condition and ready to give them a walloping.' A cheer went up. 'So, no more moaning and grumbling, turn your disappointment into determination to improve and win the next few games'. Harold sat down and John Clifford got to his feet.

'Well said Harold, I couldn't have put it better myself. We will be announcing the team to play Queensland on Saturday this evening.'

The Northern Union kept their promise to the Queensland Rugby League and selected a strong team for the second meeting between the two teams.

Saturday 20th June, Brisbane

Once again, the teams delivered a fast and free flowing game to entertain another crowd of around 12,000 people. The Queenslanders actually took an early four-point lead thanks to two penalties from the boot of Henry Bolewski. The tourists soon hit back with two tries, one each for Wagstaff and Coldrick. Another penalty from Bolewski levelled the score at 6 points all. The tourists ended the half 8 points ahead, by virtue of tries for Hall and Rogers and a conversion from Thomas.

Bolewski for the home team kicked another penalty and Longstaff replied with a penalty for the tourists before two tries by Moorhouse took the visitors to a convincing 22 points to 8 victory.

It had been a bruising encounter and players from both

sides had required treatment during the game. At one point the crowd were complaining about rough play by the visitors in general and little Johnny Rogers in particular.

That evening as the managers and captain did their review of the game Harold was asked by John Clifford if he was satisfied with the team's performance.

'That's the best all round performance of the tour so far John' came the captains reply. 'I was particularly pleased with our defence. The Queensland lads threw a lot at us and to keep them try less was a good effort. And the attack wasn't bad either.'

'Wasn't bad!' exclaimed Joe Houghton. 'I thought some of the attacking play was outstanding today. Six tries against a strong Queensland representative side was a great effort.'

'I agree with Joe on this Harold. I know you're a perfectionist when it comes to our performances but that was a damn good effort today.'

'Credit where credit is due, that was a massive improvement on our earlier performances. As I said previously, I think the Aussies have done us a favour putting the test match back by a week.'

'On the matter of the dates for the test matches' Joe Houghton continued 'I have just received confirmation that the first test will take place next Saturday, replacing the planned game against New South Wales.'

'Well we were half expecting that would be the case, weren't we?' commented John Clifford.

Joe Houghton stroked his moustache with his right hand before adding 'So it's as we expected, three tests in eight days gentlemen. That's quite a challenge.'

'Aye and we've a match on the Thursday as well haven't

we' Harold pointed out. 'I just hope we stay clear of injuries. If we do, I'm confident that we'll be taking the Ashes back home.'

The effects of the late change to the first test match continued to dominate the sporting press in Australia. Not surprisingly the Brisbane and other Queensland papers were highly critical of the actions taken by their southern friends. Equally unsurprisingly the Sydney press thought the change was necessary. Old wounds were reopened. Some sections of the Queensland media reflected on the actions which took place on the previous tour by the Northern Union when some Sydney based players were rumoured to have demanded high fees to travel North for the test match. A reference no doubt to Dally Messenger who would not take several days off from his family boat yard business unless the New South Wales rugby League paid for a replacement to cover for him.

Equally unsurprising was the reaction of the Sydney press. A few of them referred back to the Australians defeat in the Brisbane test match of 1910, blaming the number of Queensland players who were selected, for the sub-standard performance by the home team.

By and large the tourists kept out of the argument, preferring to keep their heads down and continue to work hard on their fitness and combinations. One un-named source within the British camp was quoted as saying 'We know why it was done'. Implying financial reasons were behind the change and adding 'as the financial success of the tour was already secured we were anxious to play the first test in Queensland as the tour was designed to be as cosmopolitan and comprehensive as possible' effectively saying that the tourists had nothing to do with the change.

Wednesday 24th June, Newcastle, New South Wales

The managers had made no fewer than twelve changes in the team to face Newcastle, the only player from the game against Queensland to keep his place was none other than the captain, Harold Wagstaff. Since missing the first game against Metropolis (two days after his arrival in Sydney) Wagstaff had played in every game and was under pressure from the managers to take a rest. He had resisted the pressure saying he felt good and the regular game time was benefitting both his game and the team as a whole. Neither John Clifford nor Joe Houghton could argue with this point as Wagstaff had been getting rave reviews for his performances from the local press.

The game against Newcastle would be Harold's fifth in 16 days and what a triumph it turned out to be. The team put on another fine display of attacking football as they ran out comfortable winners by 35 points to 18, scoring nine tries in the process. Harold helped himself to two tries and the other try scorers were: Johnson, O'Garra, Smales, Smith, Holland, Davies and Robinson. Alf Wood returned from injury and duly landed four goals.

Harold's performance earned him the following tribute from the correspondent of the Newcastle Morning Herald and Miners Advocate *'O'Garra gave the ball to Wagstaff, and the young "wizard", as elusive as an eel, would be away, sidestepping, feinting, and fending off until the defence was pierced.'*

Injury struck the tourists yet again as Francis, the winger from Hull, was injured in the first half and could not continue. In fact, the tourists finished with only eleven men as Holland was ordered off, followed shortly afterwards by Carpenter of the home team. The tourist's line was breached three times, but this was attributed to the numerical advantage of the home team.The Northern Union players and management were in buoyant mood as they made their way to Sydney, full of confidence and ready to take on the full might of the Australian team.

The northern leg of the tour had yielded four wins from four games and a points difference of 120 points for and 44 against. The touring squad that left Newcastle were in much more positive mood than the one which had left Sydney two short weeks earlier.

The Hull winger, Alf Francis, was one of several wingers to suffer injuries. After scoring 7 tries in his first two appearances he must have caught the selectors eyes. Unfortunately the injury he suffered in the game against Newcastle kept him out of the remainder of the tour.(Courtesy Mike Baxter)

CHAPTER 14 – THE TEST SERIES

Friday 26th June, Sydney

In the days running up to the game, the prospect of another Australian win in the forthcoming first test match of the Ashes series dominated the sports pages of the Sydney newspapers. Under pressure from the local reporters Joe Houghton eventually relented and made his views regarding the rescheduling of the game known.

'Yes: it is right that we are not satisfied, but we waived our claims rather than cause friction. It was suggested that we cancel our Bathurst visit, but this we declined to do. We had no intention of penalising Bathurst people on account of an irregularity to which they were no party. We shall carry out our tour, whatever happens, in every detail.'

The reporter pressed him on the subject of allowing substitutes in case of an injury. Joe Houghton explained that the policy had been laid down by the Northern Union Committee before the party left Great Britain and that he and his co-manager, John Clifford, did not have the power to overturn the decision. Finally, in an attempt to achieve harmony and move on he added 'Let me state emphatically that while there have been differences between us and the League Committee, we hope to smooth things over. The public have treated us fairly as sportsmen. We will do our very best to return our thanks by playing our hardest to win.'

What Joe Houghton did not tell the Sydney press was that he had already arranged a meeting that evening with the Management Committee of the New South Wales League to discuss the tourist's heavy schedule over the next eight days.

The Australians had by this time named their team. There was only one change from the team that had beaten the tourists in the first two games, Henry Bolewski, of Queensland, was selected at full back and goal kicker in place of Wally Messenger. The choice caused more than a few raised eyebrows as Messenger had landed nine successful goals from nine attempts for the Metropolis in the first game against the tourists. Sid Deane would again captain the team.

The Northern Union selected a strong team with Gwyn Thomas provisionally selected at fullback even though he was still recovering from two broken ribs. The other full back, Alf Wood, had only played one match since recovering from injury and was not risked, so Billy Jarman was on stand-by in case Thomas did not recover fully. Jack Robinson and Stan Moorhouse were selected on the wings and Wagstaff and Jenkins were the centres. The powerful back line up was completed by Billy Hall and Fred Smith at half back.

The selectors had chosen a powerful pack. Holland, Coldrick and Ramsdale made up the front row, whereas the Huddersfield trio of Chilcott, Longstaff and Clark formed the back row. Huddersfield therefore provided five of the thirteen players.

When Joe Houghton met the New South Wales Management Committee that evening, he received a sympathetic response to his representations regarding the revised schedule of three test matches in eight days. They agreed that it was, indeed, a tall order for any team. They also agreed to put it to their General Committee at the next meeting, which would take place on Wednesday 1st July, to postpone the third test until after the New Zealand leg of the tour.

Houghton and Clifford were asked to keep this information to themselves until the New South Wales League made their announcement of the change to the schedule.

The Royal Agriculture Showground, Sydney. Scene of the first test match, it had a slightly smaller capacity than the SCG. (Source Wikipedia)

Saturday 27th June, Sydney
When the players woke on match day they were treated to the site of heavy rain. Good news for the tourists, and very definitely not the conditions the home team would have preferred.

Unlike the two previous games in Sydney this one was scheduled for the Royal Agricultural Society Showground which had a slightly smaller capacity. Once more, on the morning of the match, the city centre was alive with people travelling in from the districts for the big event. Australian confidence was high, most of the newspapers recognised that the tourists form had improved but felt that the Australian team would be too strong for them.

The tourists were forced into a late change as Gwyn Thomas hadn't recovered sufficiently to take his place and Billy Jarman was called up to replace him.

The rain continued all morning but, thankfully, abated before kick-off time, when somewhere in the region of 40,000 people were crammed into the ground. Any thoughts that the British team would be rolled over for a third time were very quickly dispersed as the tourists started the game in fine form. The tourists were both sharper and stronger than their counterparts. Their dominance was eventually rewarded when Longstaff landed a long-range penalty from the half-way line. The spectators scoffed as he lined up the kick, but their derision turned to applause as the kick sailed between the posts. The visitors continued to dominate, and a fine attacking movement was completed by Stan Moorhouse who placed the ball down between the sticks only to see Jarman miss the simple conversion. 5 points to nil to the tourists.

The first half continued in similar fashion, the home team making laboured progress and the tourists defence holding firm before embarking on another flowing movement stretching the Australian defence to its limits. The only surprise was that the tourists failed to add to their total and the half finished with the score unchanged, 5 points to nil to the Northern Union.

The second half continued in the same vein and the tourists added to their total at regular intervals. First Clark with a try which was converted by Robinson, to take the score to 10 points to nil. Then another penalty from Longstaff, followed by a try for Robinson increased the tourist's lead to 15 points. Holland was on hand to finish off another fine handling movement and this time Robinson made no mistake with the conversion. At this point the tourists were in the lead by 20 points to nil and some sections of the crowd were stating to drift away as the game was clearly won. Late in the game Stan Moorhouse scored another brilliant try holding off several tacklers as he stretched over for a try in the corner, injuring himself in the process.

Shortly before the final whistle the Australians got on the scoresheet when Norman followed up his own kick to ground the ball and Bolewski landed the conversion. 23 points to 5 in favour of the tourists, at least the home side had escaped the ignominy of being kept scoreless.

At the final whistle as the rival players shook hands, Harold Wagstaff sought out his opposite number, Sid Deane. 'Congratulations 'Arold' Sid spoke has he held out his right hand. 'You certainly deserved it today.'

'Thanks Snowy, I thought the score line flattered us a bit today, you really made us work hard for the win.' Typical Wagstaff, never one to brag and generous in his praise for the losing side. The two captains walked off the pitch together with Wagstaff wrapping his right arm around the shoulders of his dejected friend.

Harold was the last to arrive in the victorious away dressing room. As he entered there was a massive roar from the rest of the squad. What a difference a win makes thought Harold. He made his way over to his good friend Stan Moorhouse who, along with Fred Longstaff, was laid out injured when the final whistle blew. 'How is it Stan?'

Stan winced, 'Not good 'Arold, I think I've done my ribs' came the reply. 'They're taking me up to the hospital to get some X-rays. I won't be playing on Monday, that's for sure.'

Harold patted him on the shoulder which brought another wince from his unfortunate friend. 'Sorry Stan. Hopefully it will be a bit easier when you get it strapped.'

Harold turned his attention to Fred Longstaff 'Nice penalties Fred, well played.'

'Thanks 'Arold, d'you know I could hear them Aussie spectators laughing when I lined that first one up. I thought I'll show you buggers how we kick in the Northern Union. I knew as soon as I hit it that it was goin' over.'

'You took a knock as well didn't you Fred, how are you feeling now?'

'I'm a bit sore, we'll have to see how it is in the morning, but it's touch and go for Monday's match'.

That's two doubtful for Monday thought Harold, I just hope everyone else is alright. Harold continued his round of the changing room congratulating each of the players in turn. Not surprisingly he was the last to make it to the communal bath, where he joined his happy friends who unceremoniously ducked his head under the water.

Fred Longstaff landed two penalties in the first test but picked up an injury which would keep him out of the next two tests. (Courtesy Huddersfield RL Heritage).

Later on, in the changing rooms Harold was taking his time getting dressed and all the other players had already left the changing room when John Clifford came in. 'Oh, you're still here then Harold. I've been looking all over for you.'

'You should know me by now John, I like to take my time. It gives me time to reflect on the game, y'know get my thoughts together before I have to answer all the questions from the reporters.'

'Aye, well there's a bunch of 'em outside waiting for you.'

'It's only to be expected, they can be a right pain in the arse at times, but I suppose they're only doing their jobs same as the rest of us.'

'Great win today Harold, there was only one team in it.'

'Aye well we're only half-way there, John. I won't be celebrating until the jobs done. Those Aussies will be hurting, just like we were a few weeks ago. They'll be up for it on Monday, no doubt about it.'

'We're going to have to make some changes now that Stan's out of contention, so we'll meet in the hotel this evening to do a review and pick the team for Monday.'

By the time evening came around the euphoria of the days win had started to settle. The players had been allowed a couple of pints to relax and celebrate their win but were under instructions to take the evening easily. A light training session was planned for the following morning when the team for Monday would be announced.

In the hotel lounge the two managers sat down with the captain for the review and selection meeting. Joe Houghton started the ball rolling. 'That was the best performance of the tour today Harold. How did you feel it went?'

'I agree with your assessment Joe, we were good today' Harold responded. 'But there were a couple of things which we need to improve on.'

John Clifford looked surprised. 'What did you have in mind Harold? I thought we were pretty good in both attack and defence today.'

'Yes, the defence was good, apart from the last few minutes when we relaxed a bit as the match was already won. Attacking wise' he paused 'I thought we should have scored more points than we did with all the good field position and chances that we had. We really should have had the game tied up by half time. The good thing was we were creating lots of opportunities, unfortunately we didn't convert enough of them into points.'

'Five tries in a test match, is a good effort though isn't it?' Joe Houghton responded.

'Yes, that's right Joe, I just think we should have made more of the opportunities which we created. But there were some other things which bothered me. For instance, all those penalties, especially at the scrum. I don't know how many there were, but the referee seemed to be blowing his whistle every two minutes, and mainly against us.'

John Clifford interrupted 'I can tell you exactly how many there were 'cos one of the reporters was keeping a running total. Would you believe there were 42 altogether and 28 of them were against us.'

'That's unbelievable, 42 penalties in a single game' Joe Houghton was amazed. 'That must be some sort of record.'

Harold did the sums. 'Well if we had 28 that means the Aussies must have only had 14 against them.' 'In other words, we gave them valuable field position far too much for my liking. Most of them were at the scrum weren't they. Fortunately, the Aussies weren't on song to-day, but I don't think we'll get away with giving them so much possession in the next match.'

'You're right Harold, most of the offences were at the scrum and also at the play the ball' John Clifford explained. 'We've got the same referee on Monday, so we need to do something to reduce the number of penalties.

Unfortunately, we don't have much time, do we?'

As usual Harold had already taken action to deal with the problem. 'I've spoken to Douglas Clark and Percy Coldrick and they're going to do some work with the forwards on their scrummaging tomorrow. One final area for improvement is on our goalkicking. Fred Longstaff landed a couple of beauties, but we missed some easy ones as well. We could do with a reliable goal-kicker in the team. On another day the goals we missed could have meant the differences between winning and losing.'

'We've already said that there's going to be at least one change to the team with Stan definitely out, but there's a couple of other players who are doubtful' John Clifford pointed out.

'Who are you referring to John?' Joe Houghton asked. 'Fred Longstaff and Bert Jenkins that I know of, they both picked up knocks' John Clifford replied, then added 'But there may be more. As we all know sometimes an injury doesn't show until the morning after.'

Stan Moorhouse injured his ribs whilst scoring his second try late on in the game. The injury would keep him out of the remaining tests. He did recover, however, and went on to be the top try scorer with 19 tries in all. (Courtesy Huddersfield RL Heritage).

'Right enough. Why don't we wait till after the run out tomorrow before we pick the team' the suggestion came from Harold and the two managers nodded in agreement.

Harold decided it was time for him to get some rest and left the pair chatting away in the lounge. Once Harold was out of earshot Joe Houghton leaned forward and spoke in a low voice. 'As you know I'm not at all happy with the schedule this week John. We've got a few injuries already if we pick up a couple more we're going to struggle at the weekend.'

'But I thought you said that the league has already agreed to downgrade the game haven't they? Saturday's match won't be a full test match will it?'

'Remember Mr Larkin, the League Secretary said they would recommend downgrading the match from a full test match. As far as I know the final decision won't be taken till Wednesday, and they haven't gone public yet with the change, have they?'

'I've seen nowt in the papers about it that's for sure. What have you got in mind Joe?'

'Well if there's nowt in tomorrow or Monday's papers about the match being downgraded I'm going to speak to Mr Larkin again and make sure the test match is off. If we lose on Monday, God forbid, the third test is going to be the decider. I for one don't want us going into that game short of players. And, d'you know what? I don't think the Aussies would want that either, they would want to beat us fair and square.'

John Clifford looked surprised, particularly with the last statement 'Well, I have my doubts on that score Joe. But you're right we should have it out with them.'

Sunday 28th June, Sydney

John Clifford and Joe Houghton watched with interest as the players were put through a few light exercises to loosen them up from the previous day's exertions. Fred Longstaff and Bert Jenkins stayed behind at the hotel to avoid aggravating their niggling injuries.

They discussed the various options for replacing them.

They came to the conclusion that Gwyn Thomas would return at full back, thus releasing Billy Jarman to replace Longstaff and the other Billy, Billy Hall, could switch from half back to fill Jenkins role in the centre. Johnny Rogers, who had been in fine form throughout the tour would come in at half back. Frank Williams was the natural replacement for Stan Moorhouse on the wing. When the light training session finished John Clifford called the trio of replacements over along with the trainer, and told them the good news. The four of them went back onto the training ground to do some more work.

Back at the hotel, after the training session had finished, John Clifford announced the team for Monday's game.

Joe Houghton took over 'I'd just like to tell you all that, following representations from myself the New South Wales League has agreed to put back the third test match until after the New Zealand leg of the tour. It will take place, therefore, on 15th August in Melbourne. Next Saturday's fixture will now be against New South Wales.'

'What's the difference though, New South Wales provide just about the whole test team?' asked Billy Davies.

'That's certainly true Billy' came the response from Joe Houghton, 'the difference is it will not be a test match and therefore the result will not count towards the Ashes.'

'So, that's official then is it Mr Houghton' Harold always used the formal term of address to the managers in front of the other players.

'Apparently it must go before the General Committee for confirmation, but they don't expect any opposition. Hopefully there will be an announcement in the papers tomorrow'.

After the meeting Harold approached Joe Houghton

'What was the logic Joe in asking for the postponement?' he asked. 'We're in tip top form at the moment, who knows what shape we'll be in after the New Zealand trip.'

Joe Houghton looked around to check that no reporters were nearby and spoke in a low voice, 'I'm concerned about the injury situation Harold. If we pick up a couple more tomorrow in key positions, we could be struggling to put out a strong team. And we have a trip to Bathurst on Thursday as well. The Ashes maybe at stake, I don't want to take that risk.'

'I can see where you're coming from Joe. Nobody wants to win the Ashes more than me, I'm just not sure a delay is the right thing.' Harold thought for a moment before adding 'Anyway, the decision has been made and I will back it to the best of my abilities, you can count on that.'

'I never doubted it for a minute Harold.'

Monday 29th June, Sydney

At breakfast that morning the two managers, John Clifford and Joe Houghton, were the first to arrive. John Clifford had a copy of the Sydney Daily Telegraph in his hands and a big smile on his face.

'What's so amusing then John?' Joe asked.

'I'm just reading this article. You know how we were ridiculed by the press after the Metropolis game?'

'Aye, I'm hardly going to forget that in a hurry, am I?'

'Well, it's the Aussies turn this time. Just listen to this.' He proceeded to read from the paper.

'The headline is simple "*HUMBLED*" then it goes on like this "*A party of Englishmen from Lancashire and Yorkshire picnicked at the Agricultural Ground, Moore Park, on Saturday. They went there ostensibly to play a rugby match against the chosen of Australia, but, finding the opposition lamentably weak they gambolled with the virility of delighted school-*

*boys and when the master called them from their play found
they had a credit balance of 23 points to 5. In the light of what
happened forty thousand people went home wondering why
the score was not 123 points to 5.''*

John Clifford couldn't supress a laugh. 'It's nice that
someone else is getting some stick from the Sydney
papers for a change.'

'Let's hope that it's more of the same in tomorrow's
papers' added Joe. 'We'd better make sure that none of
the lads see that article, they might get a bit too cocky.'

'Anyway John, never mind the funny stuff, have they
gone public about Saturday's match? That's what we
need to know.'

'Aye they have Joe. It's here right down at the bottom
of the article. I'll read it to you. *"Following representations
made by the English Managers, the Management Committee
of the League has decided to recommend that the third test
match be played in Melbourne. The Englishmen felt that the
strain of three test matches in the one week was too much,
especially when another match, involving a trip to Bathurst,
had also to be played. The general committee is certain to
agree, so that today's game will be the last test in Sydney"*.
That's sounds clear enough doesn't it?'

'Well, I'm very relieved to hear that John. Mind you,
Harold wasn't so sure it was the right thing to do. He
thought we should go for it now as we're in top form.'

Whilst John Clifford was reading the article with the
paper widespread, his two arms apart, Joe Houghton had
spotted the headlines on the front page. 'Anyway John,
what's that about a murder in Sarajevo?'

'How d'you mean Joe?'

'Haven't you seen the front pages of that paper you're
reading?'

'No, why? I just went looking for the sports page for the match reports.'

'Well there's going to be trouble. It's the heir to the Austro-Hungarian Empire – it says he's been shot by a terrorist in Sarajevo.'

'And where the 'ells Sara' he hesitated 'whatever you said then?'

'It's Sa-ra-je-vo John' he spoke the name very deliberately as if he was talking to a child. 'I think it's somewhere in the Balkans. Don't you follow world affairs John?'

'I've no time for all that politics and what 'ave you. I've got enough on my plate with rugby.'

'Here give me that paper, let me study it' Joe Houghton grabbed the newspaper. After a few minutes he continued. 'There's not much detail in the morning edition, but I don't like the sound of it. Trouble has been brewing down there for a good few years now. The Kaiser is getting too old to run that great big empire and this fellow who was killed, the Archduke, is his nephew and he was going to take over when the old man died.' Joe Houghton obviously knew a bit about the Balkans.

'Aye well what's happening in Sa-ra-je-vo' he mimicked his friend as he pronounced the name of the city deliberately, 'doesn't affect us though does it, so why should we worry about it?'

'Well I hope you're right John, but I've got a funny feeling that we'll be hearing more about this AND it very well might have an effect on all of us.'

At this point a couple of the players came into the dining room so Joe Houghton looked at John Clifford and put a finger to his mouth. John nodded in agreement and the conversation quickly went back to rugby.

As expected after their poor showing, the Australians made six changes to their team for the second test. Of the seven backs selected for Saturday's game no fewer than four of them were replaced as the Australian selectors rang the changes. Tidyman, Frawley, Wally Messenger and Fraser were the new faces in the back line. In the forwards Cann and Craig replaced Watkins and McCue.

The Northern Union team remained confident even though they had also been forced to make several changes, in their case it was due to injuries rather than form.

On a bright sunny day another big crowd was expected. On this occasion the crowd were making their way to the Sydney Cricket Ground, the same venue where the tourist had been comprehensively beaten at the start of the tour.

As the two teams lined up in the tunnel before the match, Harold Wagstaff and Sid Deane, rivals but friends, shook hands but no words were spoken. As the teams emerged from the tunnel, they were greeted by a massive cheer from the 50,000 spectators. As Harold looked around the arena all he could see was a continuous sea of faces all cheering the two sides. Harold took a deep breath as the referee called the captains to the centre for the toss. For a second time Deane and Wagstaff shook hands and then each shook the hand of the referee. 'Good luck, gentlemen' referee Tom McMahon wished the captains of both sides.

The game started at an electric pace as each side struggled to get on top. The tourists took an early lead through a penalty from Johnny Rogers and he repeated the feat a few minutes later to give the visitors a 4 point lead. In between these two scores Wagstaff had received attention for a knock to the head but after treatment was deemed alright to continue.

Gwyn Thomas's sole test appearance was in the second test. He would tour again in 1920 as vice-captain to Harold Wagstaff. (Courtesy Huddersfield RL Heritage).

The game was being played at a fast and furious pace and the play swung from end to end. The Australians made a tactical change and pulled Cann out of the pack to play as an extra half back to good effect. Eventually the deadlock was broken as Williams picked up a loose ball on the Australian 25 yard line and fed Rogers who immediately released Coldrick to score at the corner. Rogers failed with the difficult kick, but the Northern Union were ahead by 7 points to nil.

In the first game the referee, Tom McMahon Snr, had awarded penalties at regular intervals and he continued to do so in this match. Messenger had several unsuccessful attempts at goal before eventually landing one to reduce the deficit to five points. It was all Australia as the half time whistle approached, fast flowing football saw the ball travel from right to left and eventually Fraser spotted a gap, kicked through and touched down. When Messenger kicked the conversion it was all square, 7 points all as the half time whistle blew

The second half continued in entertaining fashion, on one occasion Deane was almost through the tourist's defence but Wagstaff was equal to the situation and dragged him down with a fine tackle.

The attacking play from both sides was impressive. The

fact that no points were added was due to the tackling which was particularly keen. Jack Robinson, who had been having a fine game, was the unfortunate recipient on one occasion resulting in him leaving the field with a suspected broken collar bone. The tourist's bad luck with injuries had struck again as they had to play the remainder of the game with twelve men. The versatile Jarman once again showing his adaptability by moving to the wing in place of Robinson.

It was a crucial stage of the game as both sides were threatening to take the lead. Eventually the Australians were able to take advantage of their numerical superiority and Burge scored a try which Messenger converted to put them into the lead by 12 points to 7. The visitors, although a man down, refused to give up and Smith, Rogers and Wagstaff all made valiant efforts to break the home defence but to no avail.

The Australians played conservatively in the last few minutes, keeping the ball tight and held on to their lead and, thus the series was levelled, one game all and one to play. Would the fans have to wait six weeks to see the much anticipated decider take place?

Harold was the first to congratulate Sid Deane after the whistle blew. As they shook hands, he graciously acknowledged the Australian win 'Well done Snowy, you deserved the win today.'

'Thanks 'Arold, you boys were a bit unlucky again with injuries. Jack Robinson didn't look too good I hope it isn't too bad. But you took a bad hit in the first half yourself, didn't you? Are you alright?'

'Oh me? I'm fine now but I did see stars at the time.'

'You take it easy 'Arold, I've had a few of those head knocks and it can get you later.'

The two of them walked off the field together and headed for their respective changing rooms. One would be full of smiling faces, the other would not. For the only time on the tour Harold did not make himself available to the press for an after the match interview. Billy Davies, the tour vice-captain, who hadn't played in the match filled in for him. Davies thought that the loss of Robinson was the turning point in the game as the scores were level at the time. He also pointed out that the referee, Tom McMahon, had been 'continuously cautioning' Duggie Clark throughout the game, whilst Clark had no idea what he was doing wrong.

As the defeated touring team made their way back to the hotel after the game, they heard the paper boys who were selling the evening edition shouting out that an Austrian Duke had been murdered in Sarajevo. None of the players took much notice at the time but in due course they would all come to appreciate the significance of this event in a far-away corner of Europe.

CHAPTER 15 –
THE DECIDER –
TO PLAY OR NOT
TO PLAY THAT IS
THE QUESTION

Tuesday 30th June, Sydney

The following morning there was an article in the Sydney Morning Herald with the headline '*English Captain Injured*'. The article itself explained that Harold Wagstaff had been ordered to bed for complete rest after taking a heavy kick to the head in the first half of the game, resulting in a mild concussion. However, he was expected to make a complete recovery after a few days rest.

The victory by the Australian team was welcomed in the sports pages of the Sydney press and the players were commended on the improvement they had made from their previous display. There was very little euphoria however, as most of the papers recognised the significance of the touring team playing for most of the second half with only twelve men. Some even suggested that the Northern Union would have won had it not been for Robinson's early retirement.

Reports on the test match commanded the headlines on the sports pages but the front pages were dominated by the assassination of the Archduke Franz Ferdinand in Sarajevo and the general outrage which this had created. This single event is generally accepted as being the flash point which tipped the whole of Europe into the Great War but, apart from Joe Houghton, none of the touring party was aware of its significance at the time.

Archduke Franz Ferdinand was the nephew of the Austro-Hungarian Emperor, Franz Joseph and was being groomed by his uncle to succeed him. The Emperor was growing old – he was 83 at the time of the assassination – and feeble. What's more the Austro-Hungarian Empire (also known as the Hapsburg Empire) was also in decline, a situation that Archduke Franz Ferdinand intended to address when he took over.

But why was the heir apparent to the Austro-Hungarian Empire and his wife in Sarajevo? And why choose the 28th of June to make is tour of the city?

Those players who had played the previous day were given a day off to recover whilst all the players who had not played in the test match were put through their paces at a training session.

With the injury toll mounting the team to travel up to Bathurst to play the Western Territories side included four of the players who had appeared in the second test match. Billy Hall, Johnny Rogers, Frank Williams and Billy Jarman were the players in question. Hall and Jarman would be playing their third game in six days. The team would make the 200 kilometre journey on the Wednesday and arrive back on Friday. Both Joe Houghton and John Clifford would travel with the squad leaving the other players in Sydney. Harold, who, after a full day's bed rest, had made a full recovery from his head knock would supervise light training sessions on the Wednesday and Thursday.

After a tortuous journey inland to Bathurst in dreadful weather the tourists received a warm welcome. On Thursday morning a Civic Reception in their honour took place where they were welcomed by the Mayor, Alderman H C Beavis. In the evening they were entertained at a 'Smoke Social'[18] at the Oddfellows Hall, a jovial affair with entertainment. The tourists joined in enthusiastically and Billy Jarman entertained the guests with his humorous ditties and John Smales and Alf Wood also performed solos.

In between these two social events the tourists did the entertaining with a thrilling display of rugby football in dreadful conditions, scoring ten tries in all in a 42 points to 3 victory. At one point in the second half they ran in five tries in a ten-minute spell. Billy Hall lead the way with three tries whilst O'Garra, Davies and Johnson helped themselves to two tries apiece and Williams also crossed. Wood and Guerin scored two goals each and further goals were added by Johnson and Rogers. Dawson scored a late consolation try for the home team.

Whilst the touring team were making hey on and off the field in Bathurst things were happening in Sydney.

The Sydney sporting public had gone rugby mad; they had witnessed their favourites get hammered in the first test, only to see them hit back and win a close game two days later. When the news sank in that the third and final test – the Ashes decider – would not be played in Sydney after all, and was delayed by nearly six weeks, there was consternation, disappointment and outright anger amongst them. The press too, expressed amazement and questioned the wisdom of the decision. The pressure on the New South Wales League was immense. Hardly surprising then that the meeting of the General Committee which took place on the Wednesday evening decided to review the decision. After a long and heated debate what should have been a 'rubber stamp' of the Management Committee's recommendation turned into a reversal of the decision.

News travels fast and a reporter for the National Advocate in Bathurst raised the issue with John Clifford after the game on Thursday. When the reporter told him that the new South Wales League had decided that the Test Match would go ahead on Saturday, Mr Clifford was reported as saying 'There will be no test match in Sydney on Saturday'. Contacting a colleague in Sydney the reporter relayed Clifford's response which the colleague then put to none other than the Secretary of the New South Wales League, Mr Larkin. The Secretary's response was 'If the Northern Union do not play, they should pack up and go home.'

The situation had reached crisis point so the New South Wales League took the unprecedented step of cabling the committee of the Northern Union in England with, of course, their version of events. By the time Joe Houghton and John Clifford had made their weary way back to Sydney the story was all over the newspapers. The headline in the Sydney Morning Herald read "*ENGLISHMEN WONT PLAY – TOO MANY INJURIES*". The future of the tour hung in the balance.

The two managers were caught between the proverbial rock and a hard place. Climb down, with the consequential loss of face or stick to their principles and put the entire tour at risk. Not to mention the issues for the long-term relationship with the New South Wales League. Fortunately, the decision was taken out of their hands. Several newspapers were running articles which quoted from a telegram to the Managers from the President of the Northern Union which read "*We confidently anticipate that the best traditions of the Northern Union Football will be upheld, and that you will expend every atom of energy and skill you possess to secure victory, failing which you shall lose as sportsmen*"

The normally calm John Clifford was livid. He turned to Joe Houghton 'How the hell have the press got hold of this private telegram before we have even had chance to read it ourselves? It's disgraceful!'

Fortunately, Joe Houghton remained calm. 'Let's get back to the hotel and read the telegram ourselves, the press may have got the wrong end of the stick. After all it wouldn't be the first time would it John?'

John Clifford took a deep breath, 'Yes Joe, you're right. There's no point jumping to conclusions until we have seen it for ourselves.' He paused 'But if this is a true and accurate account of the telegram, I will have no option but to tender my resignation.'

Joe Houghton raised his hands with the palms facing his friend and co-manager. 'We must keep a cool head here John, the whole tour is at stake. We can't just throw away all the hard work we and the lads have put in. I know you're upset, and so am I but we have a responsibility to the players and all the folk at home who are following our progress over here. We must keep a clear head and not get drawn into doing something hasty that we'll regret later.'

John Clifford considered what his friend had said. 'You're right Joe, the tour is too important to risk. But

I'm so angry at the way the League here have gone behind our backs while we were away in Bathurst flying the flag for the game over here.'

'I understand exactly how you feel but we must not let our hearts rule our heads on this.'

John Clifford took a deep breath and studied for a moment. 'You're right of course, but I think I'll leave the diplomacy to you on this one and I'll take a back seat. I'm afraid I might say something which we'd both regret.'

When they reached the hotel Harold and the other players were waiting to welcome them back and congratulate them on their performance against the Western Territories. Harold pulled the managers to one side. 'Have you read the papers this morning gentlemen? There's something you need to see.'

Joe Houghton put his hand on Harold's shoulder 'Yes we have Harold, it's a bit of a mess but we'll get it sorted out. Is there a telegram waiting for us?'

'Yes, it looked important, so I thought I'd better have a look at it.'

'Are the papers accurate then Harold?'

'Yes, they've got it word for word Joe. I didn't show anyone the telegram but the lads have seen it in the papers. I told them not to jump to any conclusions but to wait and see what you decided to do when you got back.'

'And how do the lads feel about playing the test match tomorrow Harold?' the question came from John Clifford.

Harold's eyes lit up, 'We're all for it actually, can't come soon enough as far as the lads are concerned.'

Joe Houghton looked relieved as he responded, 'I'm very pleased to hear that Harold, because I don't think we have any option other than to play. The telegram from

England leaves us with no alternative.'

'Can we get everybody together now to give them the news? They're all desperate to know what's going on' asked Harold.

'Why not, there's no time like the present.'

When Joe Houghton told the full squad that they would be playing the third test match on Saturday a big cheer went up and there was a huge sense of relief throughout the camp.

A final training session would take place that afternoon and the team would be named shortly afterwards when it was clear who was fit and available to play.

As the players set off for the training ground the two managers sat down to decide what to do next. Joe Houghton started the conversation. 'I will speak to Mr Larkin and tell him of our position regarding the test match. I'm sure that he will be relieved to know that we are willing to play. I shall also let him know that we are not at all happy with the way that this has been handled, and I shall leave it at that. Let's hope that the players rise to the occasion and do us proud.'

'I'm sure they will Joe, without a shadow of doubt. They've never let us down have they' came the reply. After a few seconds he smiled 'Well, apart from the first game when we got hammered but that was down to the lack of preparation time on shore, so I'm not counting that.' At which the pair of them started to laugh. It was as if all the tension which had been building up over of the last few hours was released and evaporated through their laughter.

Joe Houghton slapped his friend and co-manager on the back 'Come on John let's see how the lads are framing at training, we'll need to do a body count before the final selection wont we?'

'What about yon Mr Larkin then Joe?'

'Oh, bugger him he can wait a bit longer, let him stew a while.'

Just at that moment Harold came into the lounge. 'You two look a lot happier now what's amusing you?'

John Clifford suppressed his laughter and replied 'It's just Joe here rehearsing what he's going to say to the League secretary. Anyway, enough of the frivolity, how's your head Harold? I forgot to ask you earlier what with all the fuss and that.'

'I'm right as rain thanks, the doctor said that a couple of days rest was all I needed. I haven't done any work these last two days. I just put the lads through a few exercises, and we practiced a few moves. Tell the truth I can't wait to get out on the field tomorrow and show them Aussies a thing or two.'

So, the crisis passed, and the deciding test match of the series would go ahead as planned at the Sydney Cricket Ground, not a particularly happy hunting ground for the tourists who had lost all three games which they had played there losing a player to injury each time.

The relief in the British camp was echoed in the Australian one. They had stayed together all week and were well aware of the uncertainty surrounding the game, including the possibility of there being no game at all. The banter in the Australian camp was no doubt influenced by the newspapers who had been focusing on the number of injuries that the tourists had suffered and the effect it would have on their team.

The confidence within the Australian team was sky high, they had just beaten the tourists and were injury free. Sid Deane decided to call the group together on the

Friday evening and addressed them all. 'So, it's the test match after all lads, this is the big one, the decider. We'll have no second chances if we lose this one.'

'Yeh Snowy, but we won't lose will we guys' one of the players shouted and a chorus of agreement went up. 'They've got half their stars missing haven't they. That's why they didn't want to play us' another cheer went up.

Sid Deane held both his hands up to quell the excitement. 'Look fellas I know all these guys. I've played in their league and they are all – every single one of the twenty-six players in the squad –damn good players. What's more, we saw in the first test they've got some form together and they play as a unit. If we aren't on top of our game then they will beat us, that's for sure. They've got a big, mobile pack and they've got outstanding backs. You lads know what Wagstaff, Jenkins and Hall can do to a team, you've been on the receiving end of their play already.'

A quiet seriousness descended on the group as Deane paused in his speech.

'If we play to our potential, we can win this game and keep the ashes here in Australia, but if we aren't on our game we'll get beaten. So, let's all pull together for Australia.' This brought the biggest cheer of all from the squad.

Back at the tourist's hotel, as the two managers sat in the bar that night, Joe Houghton reflected on the day's events. 'Quite a day John, wouldn't you say?'

'I've got to hand it to you Joe, your calmness saved the day. In all the time I've been involved in the game I don't think I've ever felt so angry at the way things have been handled. In my opinion the New South Wales League have been very sneaky, sending that cable to the president of the Northern Union while we were away.'

'That was my reaction originally John, but now that things have settled down, I can see how difficult it must have been for the local league. They were getting a slaughtering in the press about delaying the match and on top of that playing it in Melbourne. What's more all the local rugby followers would have been desperately disappointed if they didn't get to see the final game of the series. Then when they made the decision on Wednesday evening, we were all up country for the Bathurst game so they couldn't contact us.'

'I suppose you're right; I can see that now. But I didn't this morning that's for sure. I don't suppose the Northern Union had much option either but to instruct us to play; nevertheless, I will be tendering my resignation when we get back home.'

'That would be a shame John, don't be too hasty. You've got plenty of time to mull it over before we get back home. Y'know all this bother, the root of the problem if you like, goes back to them not sending the Sydney players up to Brisbane for the first test up there, as it was planned in the original itinerary' added Joe.

'That actually worked out in our favour in the end, the extra preparation really benefitted the team. The Queensland League weren't happy, though were they? And quite right too. I wonder what the press in Brisbane are making of all this, I bet they're having a real go at the New South Wales League'.

How right John Clifford was. If he had been able to get hold of a copy of that day's Brisbane Daily Standard, he would have been highly amused. There was an article with the headline "SELFISH SYDNEY". In the article the reporter clearly placed the blame for the confusion on the New South Wales League. After describing the nature of the stand-off between the Northern Union and the New South Wales League the article continued *"As was the case when the breach of faith was made with Queensland over the playing of the first test match in Brisbane, the ulterior motive of the New South Wales Rugby League seems pretty clear."* The reporter went on to refer to the financial benefits of a game in Sydney versus one in Melbourne and then finished the article with this sentence *"Altogether the position reeks with unsportsmanlike tactics, so far as the New South Welshmen are concerned, at any rate".*

As Harold Wagstaff lay in bed that night, he was preparing himself for the most important game of his life. No matter how well the other games on the tour go, this is the one upon which the success of the tour will be judged. He let his thoughts drift back to his short career, the day when the farmer's dog chased him from the field just as he was about to score a try. His brief time at Underbank before being approached by the referee who recommended him to Halifax. How would his career have developed had he not been approached to join his home-town team? He remembered scoring on his debut when he was only fifteen years old. How the Huddersfield team had been strengthened by foreign stars like Edgar Wrigley and his great friend Rozzy since then. He remembered the last match he played against Salford when his Huddersfield team, with all its star players, were beaten by the dogged defence of Salford who won the Championship. Now here he was, in a posh hotel in Sydney, the night before the biggest game of the tour, which would take place in front of a large and excited crowd. This was the big one, and he was determined to do everything in his power to win it and bring home the Ashes.

CHAPTER 16 – THE DAY OF THE MATCH

Sydney 4th July 1914.

The confusion and uncertainty over the status of the match probably had an impact on the attendance, along with the poor weather. A dull, grey and wet day greeted the players as they woke that morning. Just what the tourists would have wanted.

Before the team left the hotel, John Clifford called the players into a private room where he delivered what Harold Wagstaff later described as the most moving speech he had ever heard.

'You are playing a game of football this afternoon but more than that you are playing for England, and more even than that, you are playing for right versus wrong. You will win because you have to win. Don't forget that message from home, England expects every one of you to do his duty.'

On the short journey to the ground Harold sensed a real determination amongst the players, the normal light-hearted banter was absent and had been replaced by a quiet resolve.

The reduction in spectator numbers wasn't particularly evident as the players made their way through the noisy, heaving throng of supporters as they approached the ground. Most of the newspapers had the Australians down as favourites, citing the great improvement in their performance in the second test along with the injuries that the Northern Union had sustained to some of their important players.

The sombre mood continued in the tourists dressing room. One by one the players finished their preparations; each player had his own particular set of foibles and routines. Some would leave putting on their shirt to last, others would finish by tying their laces, still others would do exercises, pushing against the changing room wall. Then they would all stand in readiness to be called into the tunnel.

As Harold made his way to the front of the group in readiness to lead them out, he saw just what effect John Clifford's speech had had and how every player was inspired by it. Most had clenched their hands into fists, others were fighting back tears; every single one of them was determined to follow the Northern Union's instructions and expend every atom of energy and skill they possessed to secure victory. Harold smiled an inner smile, confident that these friends and team-mates would not let him down in their pursuit of winning the Ashes.

The Australian team was unchanged whereas the Northern Union had made several changes due to the injury situation. The changes were mainly in the backs where Alf Wood came in for Gwyn Thomas at fullback, Willie Davies replaced Jack Robinson and Stuart Prosser was the replacement for Johnny Rogers. There was one change in the forwards as Chick Johnson replaced Billie Jarman. In the backs Billy Hall was playing his fourth match in eight days.

There was a stony silence in the tunnel as the teams

lined up, side by side. Sporting handshakes were exchanged but few words were spoken. The determination of the tourists was plain for all to see as the made their way out onto the Sydney Cricket Ground, the very same ground where they had suffered three defeats, the latest one just five days earlier. Arawa, the correspondent for the Sydney Daily Telegraph, described the entrance of the tourists most lyrically *"as the huge English team strode on to the soddened turf, there was hardly a smile amongst them; there was a grim, teeth-set determination, all over them. Just before the start several of them, in the best Irish fashion, spat upon their hands and rubbed them together. There was bound to be some dirty work at the crossroads."*

Frank Williams was injured early on in the match. He bravely continued until the beginning of the second half before he aggravated the injury and was forced to leave the field. (Courtesy Andrew Hardcastle).

The game started with both sides playing conservatively. The Northern Union's dreadful run of injuries continued as Frank Williams, in virtually his first involvement twisted his ankle badly. After a long delay he was able to continue but he was hobbling badly. The injury appeared to affect the home team more than the tourists. The referee, which once more was Tom McMahon, was again awarding plenty of penalties but this time it was mainly the Australians who were incurring his wrath. He was particularly severe on Craig and Cann who were regularly caught offside. After missing with an earlier shot at goal, Alf Wood scored the first points of the game by landing a good penalty. Two points to nil to the tourists.

The Australians made what must have been a planned tactical change, by pulling Cann out of the pack to make an additional half back. The change had the effect of weakening the home scrummage and the British team took advantage. The home team lacked the coherency and slick combinations of five days earlier and were ragged at times as the tourists continued to grind them down with their forwards beginning to dominate the home pack.

Wood had a couple more chances to increase the lead but his attempts at two difficult shots were unsuccessful. Eventually the tourists scored in slightly controversial fashion. Willie Davies, who had been selected on the wing, put a kick through and behind the Australian try line and appeared to win the chase to touch the ball down. Referee McMahon had seen an infringement by Tidyman for the defence who had obstructed Davies to prevent him from reaching the ball and awarded a penalty try. Alf Wood slotted an easy conversion over from under the posts to stretch the lead to seven points.

The game was being played at a fast pace and the teams seemed to take turns at attacking each other. The tackling and covering were up to the mark and neither side could find the vital opening. The penalties continued and Wood missed another shot at goal before landing a difficult shot from long range after Fraser had been penalised for offside. 9 points to nil to the visitors.

The play continued to ebb and flow, and the penalties continued to come at regular intervals. Following one awarded against the tourists Messenger had the chance to put the home team on the score sheet but missed badly. The Australians had a promising move stopped by the referee when he awarded yet another penalty to relieve the hard pressed British defence.

Further Australian pressure could not break down the stubborn British defence and Messenger had another opportunity from a penalty but missed again. There were no more scores before half time which ended with the Northern Union still leading by 9 points to nil.

In the dressing room Wagstaff addressed the team. 'Well played lads that was a good effort. If we keep playing the same type of football, we can win this.' He turned to the unfortunate Frank Williams 'How is it Frank?'

'Not good 'Arold but I'll keep going, fortunately I've not been called on too much.'

'Well done Frank. I'm amazed that the Aussies haven't targeted you on the flank. Right boys 40 minutes to decide the Ashes let's do it.'

The second half opened with a good attacking move from the tourists which was repelled before the Australians made their way back up field. Another clever combination was started by Wagstaff who sent Clark clear. The Huddersfield forward had broken his thumb in the first half but played on with it strapped up; as he approached the last man, Halloway, the Australian scrum half, he prepared to hand the defender off but then remembered his left hand was injured so he pulled back his arm and Halloway – quite fairly – pulled him to the ground. With all his weight now concentrated on his left side he fell heavily on his shoulder. After a few minutes of attention from the Ambulanceman he was persuaded to leave the field with a badly dislocated shoulder.

Worse was to come for the tourists, moments after

Clark had left the field Wagstaff threw a long pass out to the hobbling Williams who stepped backwards to catch it only for his ankle to give way completely. This time he was unable to continue, and he too had to leave the field. The Northern Union were now down to eleven men, surely the Australians would make their numerical superiority count?

Amazingly Clark, showing immense bravery, returned to the fray to help out his outnumbered team-mates. However, it was only to be short lived, as the first time he was involved in any action he was in excruciating pain and, once more, he was led from the field crying tears of frustration.

Even though they were down to eleven men it was the brave men of the Northern Union who scored next. Wagstaff cut through the defence and passed to Chick Johnson, now playing on the wing in place of the injured Williams. Johnson had just the full back to beat when, to everyone's surprise, he put the ball down on the floor and dribbled it past the mesmerised full back and continued to dribble all the way to the line where he dropped on it for the try. Wood kicked the conversion and the lead had now stretched to 14 points. Could the Northern Union really do it? Could they hold onto their lead with a quarter of the game still left to play?

The Australians hit back almost immediately when, from a scrum near the tourist's line, Messenger forced his way over in the corner. It was too far out for him to make the conversion. 14 points to 3 to the tourists and game on. Sensing a turning of the tide the partisan Australian crowd roared their heroes on.

The pressure on the away defence mounted but Wagstaff and Davies combined well to take play back into the home team's half. Despite their numerical advantage the Australian team were being driven back by the clever combinations of their visitors with Wagstaff in particular to the fore.

Stuart Prosser the Halifax half back made his first test appearance in the third test victory. (Courtesy Andrew Hardcastle).

Gradually numerical superiority began to count, as the Australians mounted wave after wave of attack, somehow the British defence held, sometimes by sheer willpower and sometimes by good fortune. After a flowing move Fraser had the line at his mercy only to drop the ball. Chance after chance went begging. On one occasion Sullivan received the ball a few yards from the line and could have strolled over for the try but dallied so long that he was swamped by defenders.

Misfortune continued to haunt the tourists as Hall, who had played an outstanding game, was concussed in a heavy tackle and he too had to leave the field, it was now ten against thirteen. Wagstaff seemed to be everywhere. One minute he was in the scrum helping his depleted forwards, the next he was setting up an attack and then putting his body on the line to stop another attack. The whole team responded to his example by throwing themselves into tackles and supporting each other. None more so than Stuart Prosser, the little half back, who suddenly broke through the defence from near his own line on a lone charge. Another try for the tourists was in the offing, as two team-mates were up in support, but he was brought down by Hallett and lost the ball in the mud just inside the Australian half.

Time and again the home team drove at the opposition line. Somehow the Northern Union defence kept the Australians at bay. The crowd, appreciating the bravery of the visitors began to switch their allegiance. Every tackle, every kick, every half break by the visitors was cheered enthusiastically by the crowd. The clock ticked down, and the Australians became more anxious. When clear heads and calmness were needed, they were nowhere to be found.

Just before the final whistle the Australian captain, Sid Deane, did manage to cross for a try. Messenger capped a miserable day for his kicking by missing an easy conversion. Tom McMahon blew his whistle one last time and the game was over. The brave men of the Northern Union had pulled off the most amazing victory against the odds. The Ashes had been won in the most dramatic game ever seen in Australia or anywhere else for that matter.

As the players made their weary way from the pitch Wagstaff was besieged by well-wishers, desperate to shake him by the hand and congratulate him. He had led his team magnificently and they had responded with a performance of immense bravery and courage. Sid Deane, his opposite number, was one of the first to congratulate him. The series over the two men embraced each other, they had fought like demons but now they were sportsmen, friends who admired and appreciated the skills and efforts of each other.

Arthur 'Chick' Johnson scored the tourists second try to open up a fourteen point lead. The Widnes forward had been moved to the wing when Frank Williams was injured. He also scored a vital try in the test match against New Zealand. (Courtesy Steve Fox).

The Northern Union dressing room was a scene to behold, it looked more like a war time army hospital. The ambulance men were working overtime as players were being bandaged and cuts were being stitched. The grim faces of five days earlier had been replaced by smiles and cheering as the players celebrated the victory.

The two managers strode into the room and another cheer went up. John Clifford's normally clear voice was choked with emotion as he simply said, 'Well done lads, you've done us all proud.'

CHAPTER 17 – A LEGEND IS BORN THE RORKES DRIFT TEST MATCH

4ᵗʰ July, Sydney

The gentlemen of the press, having witnessed one of the finest games ever played, were desperate for quotes to include in their columns the following day.

While the players were recovering and celebrating in the dressing room Mr H. Flegg, one of the Australian selectors was fulsome in his praise of Wagstaff's wonderful team. 'Their play in the second half was a revelation and their pluck in the circumstances was remarkable. I am not going to criticise any individual member of the Australian team. All I can say is they met their masters and were fairly and squarely beaten by a team who for half of the game only played 11 men. I congratulate Wagstaff and his men on their wonderful performance.'

Sid Deane, captain of the beaten Australians was equally magnanimous 'There is very little room for criticism as we were hopelessly beaten for and aft. They outclassed us. Wagstaff played a wonderfully good game. The defence of the Englishmen in the second half was the finest I have ever witnessed.'

When Harold Wagstaff emerged, tired but triumphant, he too was generous in his praise for the opposition. 'Tell the Sydney public that it was the hardest game of my life. I am naturally overjoyed at leading England to victory against such great odds. We had to fight tremendously hard but the game, though vigorous, was never vicious, and the injuries to my men were quite accidental. The large crowd gave us a great reception and treated us generously, not only in today's game but right through our series of games in Sydney. We won today but I must congratulate Sid Deane and his men on the big fight they put up.'

Sid Deane had waited patiently as Harold gave his little speech to the reporters. Once the interview was over and the reporters had started to leave, anxious no doubt to get their articles in for publishing he walked over to Harold and they shook hands again. 'That was quite a performance you put in today 'Arold. At one time I though there must have been at least three of you, you were everywhere.'

'That's very generous of you Snowy, but it was a team performance really. I just did my best as I always try to.'

'You're too modest 'Arold, you were sensational. The papers will be singing your praises tomorrow.'

'Aye well I'm not one to be swayed by what the papers say. It's not that long since they were rubbishing us after those first two games. Anyway, enough of me I hear we're going to be meeting again next year. Is it true that you're off to Hull to play with Billy Batten and Herb Gilbert?'

'We've still got a few details to iron out, but yes it looks like we'll be locking horns again. That's if there isn't a war by then.'

'Are you referring to that bother in the Balkans, the one where some German guy got shot?'

Sid couldn't help but laugh. 'You're a great footballer 'Arold but you don't know much about current affairs, do you. It was an Austrian Archduke, heir to throne, it wasn't some nondescript German bloke!'

'Hells bells Snowy, we've been concentrating that much on playing rugby we haven't had time to study the papers. I'll pick up a paper tomorrow and see what all the fuss is about. Most of the guys are sailing for New Zealand tonight, but the rest of us don't leave until next Wednesday. It'll be the first few days of rest I've had on this tour.'

'Good luck with the voyage and well done. I'll see you up in Yorkshire.'

'Yeah, don't forget to pack your overcoat, it's bloody cold in Hull.'

Sid Deane, who had been given the nickname 'Snowy' due to the colour of his hair, gave an involuntary shiver as he waved goodbye to his friend and rival.

The team managers had decided to split the squad into two groups for the journey over to New Zealand. With a four-day trip to Wellington, the New Zealand capital, across potentially choppy waters ahead of them, they took a group of fifteen players from whom the team would be selected for the first game seven days later. The evening boat from Sydney had actually delayed its departure to fit in with the finish of the game.

With part of the team booked to sail to New Zealand for the next leg of their tour that evening there was no time for celebrations and no reception in the mayor's parlour. That didn't lessen the spirits of the team though; they may have been physically *down under* but mentally they were very definitely on top of the world.

The group who sailed that evening on the Ulimaroa was made up as follows: Thomas, Williams, Hall, Davies, O'Garra, Smith, Prosser, Guerin, Jarman, Johnson, Smales, Chilcott, Roman, Holland and Clampitt. Joe Houghton was in charge and David Murray the team's local trainer travelled with them.

The remaining players would travel later by boat direct to Auckland. They would then make their way to meet the rest of the squad in Napier for the game against Hawkes Bay.

Monday 10ᵗʰ July, Sydney

The players who had remained in Sydney were Wagstaff, Rogers, Moorhouse, Robinson, Longstaff, Clark, Jenkins, Ramsdale, Francis, Coldrick and Wood, most of whom were injured or nursing knocks. They were granted a few days off to recover from their hectic programme before their departure for Auckland later that week.

After a complete rest on Sunday, Harold woke early on Monday morning. It was too early for breakfast, so he decided to take a relaxing walk around Sydney in the hope of picking up a newspaper. Even though he, like the rest of the squad, was in a state of elation due to their victory on Saturday, he was decidedly uneasy about the threat of war that Sid Deane had mentioned to him and determined to find out what was going on.

As he turned a corner, he could hear a newspaper boy shouting the headlines 'Australians beaten in final test. England finish with ten men.' Harold blushed shyly as he fished around in his pocket for some change to pay the lad for the paper; it was the Sydney Daily Telegraph. He slowly made his way to the local park where he sat down to read the paper. He ignored the headlines on the front page as he quickly found his way to the sports column where he found what he was looking for.

The headline read 'The English Eleven – How they won the rubber'. Underneath the main headline was a phrase that would be used to describe the test match in years to come. 'Arawa', the pen name of the Daily Telegraph's correspondent, drew the comparison between the plucky defence of the Northern Union try line with the heroic defence of Rorke's Drift in the Zulu war. The bravery shown at the defence of Rorke's Drift in 1879 had led to no fewer than eleven Victoria Crosses being awarded.

As Harold continued to read the article, he began to realise just how amazing the team's performance two days earlier had been. The reporter was obviously something of a history buff as the article also drew comparisons with the Duke of Wellington, the Battle of Inkerman and even Richard the third got a mention. The reporter was glowing in his praise of the British team's performance and of Wagstaff in particular.

Harold closed the newspaper and folded it up. He placed it under his arm and set off back to the hotel. When he arrived at the hotel, breakfast was being served. He quickly made his way to the table where John Clifford was sitting.

'Ah there you are Harold, I thought you must have been having a lie in.'

'Me? No John I'm not one for lying in bed. I was up early so I thought I'd take a look around town.'

'Is that today's paper you've got there Harold?'

'Aye it is.'

'What's it got to say about the match then? Have they been giving the Australians another rollicking?'

'Well, sort of, he hesitated. 'It's more about us actually. The fella', you know the reporter, has given us quite a write up actually. It's a bit embarrassing really.'

'How d'you mean Harold? Pass it here, let me have a look.'

While John Clifford read the article, Harold helped himself to a cup of tea. Clifford gasped at times as he read the report. 'Well, well, well. Quite the historian, isn't he.' As he finished reading the report, he carefully closed the newspaper and put it down on the table.

'See what I mean John. Embarrassing isn't it?'

'I'll grant you that his language is a bit flowery but he's only telling the truth Harold. The way you and the lads stuck to it against the odds was truly remarkable. I don't know how you did it, I really don't. It was as if the Aussies had been drugged or hypnotised. The harder they tried the worse they got. I lost count of the number of times they seemed certain to score and then one of the lads would pop up – as if by magic – and tackle them, right in the nick of time. Either that or they would drop the ball.'

'I suppose you're right. I was too busy tackling to notice their mistakes during the game, but I was thinking last night about the three tests. I reckon we were pretty good in all three, might have won the second one as well if Jack hadn't been injured. But the Aussies were poor in the first and third but good in the second one. Even Wally Messenger, who's probably the best goalkicker in the world, was off form. He landed eight out of eight when we played Metropolis but couldn't land a single one on Saturday and he had some relatively easy ones. It's weird isn't it?'

'One thing's for sure Harold, that test match is going to go down in history.' John Clifford paused for reflection 'Fancy comparing the match to a battle in the Zulu war. They awarded a load of VC's, I forget how many. Happen we should give you all a medal as well.'

'Nay John don't be daft. It was only a game of football.'

'I think I'll give it a bit more thought and have a chat with Joe about it when we meet up next week. Anyway, how are you feeling now, you took a few knocks didn't you?'

'Oh, I'll be fine after a few days rest John. I'll be honest I'm pleased that I wasn't asked to go on that first boat to Wellington. How come they've taken Frank Williams with 'em, surely he's not going to be fit to play next week. He was in a right bad way on Saturday, I don't know how he managed to play on as long as he did.'

'As you know Harold, we haven't a fit winger in the squad. He's going to play Jack O'Garra on one wing and I'm sure he'll do a grand job. But I don't know what he's going to do on the other. He says he has a plan up his sleeve, but he wouldn't tell me what it was. He might be hoping Chick Johnson is fit, he did right well when we moved him onto the wing on Saturday didn't he.'

'Aye he did. I wondered what the hell he was doing when he put that ball down on the ground and started dribbling. But then it was like the ball was tied to his foot. That try lifted us all, it gave us belief.'

'Right' John Clifford rose from the table. 'You and the lads enjoy your rest – you've earned it. I'm afraid I have a mountain of paperwork to catch up with. Four games in eight days and a trip up country don't leave much time for book-keeping.'

CHAPTER 18 – A
WARM WELCOME
IN NEW ZEALAND

Wellington, 8th July

Wellington, 8th July

After a smooth passage from Sydney the Ulimaroa docked at Wellington on 8th July where the squad was welcomed by the president of the New Zealand Council, Mr J Carlaw. On this occasion they did not receive a Civic Reception as the Mayor declined to entertain them due to the fact that they were professionals. Not that the tourist would have felt deprived in any way. They were given a Parliamentary reception where they were introduced to the Prime Minister of New Zealand, W F Massey, followed by a tour of the Parliamentary Buildings. That evening they were entertained at Barrett's Hotel by the Management Committee of the Wellington Rugby Football League.

The warm welcome was to be a feature of their visit to New Zealand and would be repeated throughout their tour. The tourists were enthusiastically welcomed wherever they went. The events of their tour of Australia had been widely covered in the New Zealand press and their bravery in the final test was greatly admired by the New Zealand sporting public. On the previous tour of

1910 the tourists only played matches in Auckland, the city where rugby under Northern Union rules was most widely played. This year's itinerary had been developed specifically with a view to stimulating the game in some more remote places. Not that Wellington was in any shape or form remote, it was after all, the capitol of the Dominion of New Zealand.

Once more the manager of the touring team became embroiled in the politics of where and when to play. This time it was not as serious as the test match controversy, but it still caused ill feeling in a certain part of New Zealand.

The original itinerary included a match on the South Island of New Zealand. Arrangements had been made to play a game at Christchurch on the Wednesday following the match in Wellington, however this game was cancelled as the Christchurch club decided that they weren't in a position to accommodate the tourists. The league in Christchurch had requested a Saturday fixture and, as Hawkes Bay had been granted one, were very disappointed that their game was scheduled for mid-week. They argued that it was not financially viable to play on a Wednesday as this was a normal working day for their players and spectators. Joe Houghton attended a conference with representatives of the New Zealand Council, the governing body for rugby league in New Zealand, where an agreement was reached that the touring team would come to Canterbury and play, regardless of gate and other considerations. This offer was also turned down, so the game did not take place. This was probably a relief for the touring team as they would have had to make a tiring sea journey south to Christchurch before making their way back north to Hawkes Bay.

Joe Houghton had brought a reduced squad of fifteen players with him. Three of the injured wingers, Stan Moorhouse, Jack Robinson and Alf Francis were all left behind and would travel with the remainder of the squad direct to Auckland. Frank Williams was the only recognised winger in the party that travelled to Wellington, but he was also injured and would not be fit to play at the weekend.

Jack O'Garra, the young Widnes half back, was used as an emergency winger due to the injuries to the first choice wingmen. (Courtesy Steve Fox).

Jack O'Garra, whose normal position was half back, would play on one wing but who would take their place on the other wing? As John Clifford had speculated Joe Houghton had a Plan B up his sleeve. When the team to play Wellington was announced, there was a new name of the team sheet. S B Houghton of the Napier club in New Zealand, but formerly of St Helen's, was named as the team's right winger. Desperate times call for desperate measures and Joe had obviously decided to keep it in the family.

11th July, Wellington
Despite all their injuries, the team named for the first match of the New Zealand leg of the tour was a strong one. Gwyn Thomas was at full back, Houghton and O'Garra on the wings and Wille Davies and Billy Hall occupied the centres. Stuart Prosser and Fred Smith were

the half backs and the forwards were Jarman, Chilcott, Smales, Rowan, Guerin and Clampitt.

The weather for the first game was typically English with heavy rain showers in the morning which continued on and off throughout the game. The New Zealand sporting public had been following the fortunes of the touring side in Australia and interest in the match was high. Recognising this the Wellington Rugby League had switched the venue from the small Basin Reserve ground to the much larger Newtown Park.

Joe Houghton had the pleasure of sitting with a number of local dignitaries. The Governor of New Zealand, the Earl of Liverpool, and his wife were present along with the Prime Minister, the Right Honourable W F Massey and the Mayor of Wellington, Mr J P Luke. The crowd was estimated to be in the region of 6 – 7,000 and the teams provided them with a highly entertaining game of football. Many of the spectators would have been watching their first ever game of Rugby League and the local paper commented afterwards that they could not have failed to be impressed with speed and skill shown.

The game itself was a hard-fought affair which the tourists won by 14 points to 7. The tourists scored four tries in all, including one from the local substitute, Sammy Houghton, who justified his place with a strong display on the wing. Thomas, Chilcott, and Hall scored the other tries and Guerin landed a goal.

With the planned game at Christchurch cancelled the team made their way North to meet up with their colleagues in Napier where they would play a team representing the Hawkes Bay clubs.

14th July, Auckland

When the tour had been planned it was recognised that

Northern Union rugby was still in its early days in New Zealand and Rugby Union remained strong in the Dominion. The smear of professionalism still hung over the new sport. New Zealanders were rightly proud of their union team which was recognised as the best in the world. The authorities were also worried about the drift of their top talent to the professional game. Both John Clifford and Joe Houghton would be challenged on the issue of professionalism by the press on several occasions and both would provide robust responses to the question. They would point out that all the players in the squad were working men and most of them held down manual jobs, any payment for playing was to recompense them for the time and money they lost from missing work in order to play. They also pointed out that the players were receiving only £1/10 shillings per week whilst on tour, whereas the 'amateur' New Zealand rugby union players were paid 6 shillings per day whilst on tour in Australia. The players would also share in any profits that the tour made. Bearing this in mind the managers had impressed upon the whole team that they were ambassadors for the sport and that their behaviour on and off the pitch should reflect this.

A local reporter had christened the second group of Northern Union players 'the crocks', an obvious reference to all the injuries they had suffered. As John Clifford led this group of crocks down the gang plank in Auckland the rest of the team were still in Wellington, from where they would make their way direct to Napier.

16ᵗʰ July, Napier

When the two groups were finally re-united the two managers greeted each other as long-lost friends would do, and John Clifford congratulated his co-manager on their successful visit to Wellington.

Joe Houghton responded 'The weather down there wasn't great, John, but they gave us a right royal reception. They even gave us all a tour of the Parliament buildings, and none other than the Governor AND the Prime Minister came to watch the match. Anyway, enough of that, how are the lads doing? What's the score on the injury front?'

'Harold tells me that a few of them should be fit for the weekend. They've been getting in some light training to run off the stiffness and loosen up, but we should have a decent squad to pick from, so you won't have to rope in a local lad this time.' There was just a hint of sarcasm in his voice at the reference to a 'local' lad.

'Ah, you heard about me enlisting my lad then. I had no option really. There was no way Frank Williams could have played, I had to put Jack O'Garra on the other wing as it was.'

'Well I heard he had a decent game, didn't let anyone down at all, even bagged a try, didn't he?'

'Aye John, it was a proud moment for me when he put that ball down over the line. Mind you I had to get permission from the local league before he could play, what with him being registered with the New Zealand rugby board.'

'I heard there was some confusion over a game down south, Christchurch wasn't it?'

'It was a bit of a mess really John, bit of internal politics with the New Zealand administrators. The league down in Christchurch wanted, nay expected, to get a Saturday fixture. When they found out we were due down there on the Wednesday they err, how shall I put it' he paused and scratched the back of his head with his right hand.

'Let's say they weren't happy, especially when they realised that Hawkes Bay had got a Saturday fixture.'

'What was wrong with playing the game on Wednesday then?'

'They reckoned it wasn't financially viable, what with the players and the spectators working and that. I told them that we were willing to go down there and play irrespective of the gate, but they wouldn't budge.'

'Well it probably made your life a bit easier, but they do say the South Island is very beautiful, it's a pity you didn't get to see it.'

'That's not the end of the story though. They've suggested we send a team down after the Test match in Auckland to play on the 8th August and then sail direct to Melbourne for the final game against New South Wales on the 15th.'

'That sounds a bit tight Joe, what did you say?'

'I said we'd look into it with the New Zealand Council, but like you said it's all a bit tight.'

'How did you leave it then Joe?'

'I've left it with the New Zealand chaps to work out if it really is practical for us to fit the game in, but I've told them we will need to reach Melbourne at least a couple of days before the game. I really want us to finish the tour on a high note and I'd dearly love to get one over on the New South Wales lot.'

'I'm with you on that score Joe, let's see what the New Zealand Council comes up with. It's still a few weeks off and we've got this game against Hawkes Bay coming up on Saturday and then the games come thick and fast, so we've got plenty to keep us busy.'

18th July, Auckland

Harold Wagstaff's optimism about the recovery of the

injured players was, at least in part, correctly placed and some of the injured players were available for selection.

The tourists were still short of wingers so Stan Moorhouse, who must have been a quick healer, was included on the right wing following the injury to his ribs in the first test. The tourists lined up as follows: Thomas, Moorhouse, Wagstaff, Davies, O'Garra, Prosser, Smith, Roman, Clampitt, Johnson, Guerin, Jarman and Holland.

A crowd of 6,000 were present on a beautiful sunny day and witnessed an entertaining game which the tourists won comfortably by 30 points to 7. Willie Davis completed a hat trick of tries, Harold Wagstaff added two more and Billie Jarman scored the final try. Joe Guerin landed 5 goals and Gwyn Thomas also scored a goal.

New Zealand hospitality was to the fore once again as the tourists and the home team enjoyed a civic reception and then the local MP, Mr J V Brown, invited them to attend the pantomime '40 Thieves'.

The next stop on the tour of the North Island was Taranaki which meant a journey from the west coast across to the eastern coast of the island.

Thursday 23rd July, Taranaki

The game against Taranaki was another convincing victory for the touring side. By half time the visitors had built a big lead, 24 points to 3. Hall, Smith, Wagstaff, Moorhouse (2) and Romans had all scored tries and Guerin had kicked three goals. Moorhouse was having a field day as he helped himself to three more tries in the second half and O'Garra also crossed twice. Guerin finished with five goals as the final score was 43 points to 11 in favour of the tourists.

It wasn't all good news for the Northern Union as Wagstaff picked up an injury to his chest which would keep him out of the match against Auckland in two days' time.

So, it was on to Auckland that the tourists travelled for what they expected to be the toughest test so far of the New Zealand leg of the tour,

Saturday 25ᵗʰ July, Auckland

On a showery day around 20,000 spectators made their way to the Domain, the venue for the game between the Northern Union and Auckland. The visitors took the field without their talisman and captain, Harold Wagstaff. The team chosen was, nevertheless, a strong one. Alf Wood was the last line of defence. Moorhouse and Davies were on the wings and Hall and Jenkins were the centres. Johnny Rogers and Fred Smith the half backs completed an impressive back line. The forwards were a powerful lot too with Ramsdale, Longstaff, Chilcott, Johnson, Holland and Coldrick selected.

The teams had attended a reception at the Waitemata Hotel in the morning before the game, and they would also dine there after the match. The visitors were anticipating a tough match, but they quickly raced into a 15 points lead through tries for Coldrick, Jenkins and Moorhouse, all converted by Wood. Auckland then fought their way back into the match with two penalties from Ifwerson to go in at half time trailing by 15 points to 4.

It got even better for the home side in the second half with Savoury notching a try and the lead was down to 8 points. The tourists hit back with tries from Hall and Moorhouse to restore a healthy lead for the visitors. Auckland were not done yet, and scored a try through Clarke, converted by Ifwerson. That was as good as it got for the home team as Holland, Ramsdale and Rogers all scored tries with Wood converting two of them. Final score Auckland 12 Northern Union 34. Once more the touring team had risen to the occasion and produced an impressive display of handling and running in trying conditions.

The newspapers continued to report on the rising tension in the Balkans in the aftermath of the assassination of Archduke Franz Ferdinand, but the tourists had other things on their mind. A mid-week game against Wanganui meant another long journey, to be followed by the test match against New Zealand on the Saturday.

Monday 27ᵗʰ July, Auckland

Wagstaff had recovered sufficiently from his injury to be part of the squad of thirteen players which travelled with John Clifford to Wanganui. The other twelve players were: Wood, Davies, Jenkins, O'Garra, Prosser, Rogers, Coldrick, Ramsdale, Longstaff, Guerin, Clampitt and Roman.

The group were in for a new experience as they left Auckland on Monday. They travelled overland to Taumarunui where they boarded a steamboat which would take them down river to Wanganui on the coast, where they would arrive on the morning of 29ᵗʰ July.

As the boat set sail from Taumarunui Harold Wagstaff and his vice-captain, Willie Davies stood on the deck and admired the rolling countryside. 'People reckon this area is very similar to the English countryside, what do you think 'Arold?'

Harold carefully considered this proposition as he scanned the green fields and meadows. 'I can't say as it reminds me of Holmfirth to be honest Willie, how about you?'

'I'm with you 'Arold. It's a beautiful country, New Zealand, no doubt about it. I can see why Joe Houghton's lad settled here, there's so much space and the air is so clear.'

He took a deep breath in to emphasise the point.

'I tell you what Willie, we've been away from home now for, how long? Three months isn't it, and it'll be another two afore we get back. It's a bloody long time to be away from home, but y'know I've enjoyed every minute of it. I couldn't wish to be with a better set of lads. I know we've had our share of bad luck, with the injuries and what have you, but the feeling when Tom McMahon blew that whistle in Sydney and we'd won back the Ashes...' He seemed to go off into a world of his own.

Willie Davies coughed to break the moment. 'Aye job done hey 'Arold?'

'Not quite Willie, we've done the main thing we came here to do by winning the Ashes but we've another job to do here Willie. Spread the word, show them that Northern Union Football is the best game in the world.'

A view of the town of Taumarunui showing the river in the distance (Courtesy Glenn Woodworth).

The tour programme was certainly giving the lads a good tour around the North Island and wherever they went the locals were generous in their hospitality and grateful for the visit. On this particular occasion the team were treated to a Civic Reception from the Mayor at the Council Chamber – no issues about professionalism in this outpost. They were also given a motor tour around the town and in the evening after the match they were banqueted by the ladies of the Lancashire and Yorkshire Societies at the Burlington Hotel.

Meanwhile in Europe, Austria declared war on Serbia and Austria's German Allies were sporting for a fight. Dangerous times.

Thursday 30th July, Wanganui

The way the visitors showed their gratitude for the warm hospitality they had received was to hand out a thirteen try hammering to their hosts. Jenkins was the tormentor in chief with three tries, Wagstaff, Moorhouse, Prosser and Longstaff all scored two and Guerin and Clampitt had one each, Wood kicked nine goals as they ran out winners by 57 points to 12.

Harold Wagstaff and John Clifford reflected on a job well done. 'Just one more match to go on the tour of New Zealand John', Harold started, 'so back to Auckland for the test match.'

'The New Zealanders are a determined bunch. They're proud of their rugby tradition, Harold' Clifford responded. I believe they've brought the whole squad to Auckland five days early to prepare for the game. It's another tough game to look forward to.'

'But won't it be the same team as last week when we played Auckland John? We beat them convincingly.'

'No Harold, it's not like it was in Sydney, they've selected players from all over New Zealand.'

'I'm sure our lot will be up for the challenge come Saturday. Anyway, changing the subject John, what d'you make of this here war situation with Austria and err....'

'Serbia? Joe Houghton tells me it's been on the cards ever since that Archduke was killed in Sarajevo. A lot of folk are saying we could get drawn into it an'all. I don't like it at all Harold. Here we are on the other side of the world with a six-week sea passage to look forward to.

Me and Joe have been discussing how we'll all get back if there's a war on, it could be very tricky. I just hope that the politicians can sort it out without going to a full-scale war. In fact, Joe is leaving for Sydney tomorrow to make arrangements for the return journey.'

'Ee John, I hadn't thought about it like that. D'you really think it could come to that. Some of the lads are on reserve for the army. Jack Robinson is, I know that for certain and there may be a few more. If we go to war, they'll be called up straight away.'

'Aye, well they'll have a job on won't they? They're on the wrong side of the world' he chuckled but quickly became serious again. 'It's the Germans I'm worried about; they've been building up a huge fleet of battleships. I still think our navy is the best in the world though.' There was a pause in the conversation whilst they both considered the situation. John Clifford continued 'I don't want the lads getting all agitated over this Harold, so keep it to yourself, at least until after the test match.'

'Aye John, I will. I promise.'

Saturday 1ˢᵗ August, Auckland

20,000 spectators made their way on a showery day to the Domain for the test match between the Northern Union and New Zealand. The attendance, though well short of the figures from the games in Sydney, demonstrated the level of interest in the League game in New Zealand. On the same day across the Tasman Sea New Zealand's Rugby Union side would beat Australia by 17 points to nil in front of less than 12,000 people in Brisbane.

The Northern Union had its strongest available team on duty with Wood at full back, Moorhouse and Davies on the wings and the powerful centre partners were Wagstaff and Jenkins. Hall and Smith were the half back pairing. Clampitt, Ramsdale, Longstaff, Coldrick, Johnson and Holland made up the forwards.

The match was won by the tourists by the slender margin of three points. Wagstaff declared it was the hardest match of the tour. Considering the circumstances of the third test in Sydney this statement could be attributed to Wagstaff's growing diplomatic skills. In a game of two halves the tourists were on top in the first half and led by 11 points to 3 at half time. The wingers had been in try scoring form with Moorhouse crossing twice and Davies once. Wood landed one conversion. Wilson had registered the home team's points through an unconverted try.

In the second half the New Zealanders came into their own, and when Banks scored a try which was converted the lead was down to a narrow three points. The tourists were put under tremendous pressure by the home team but, as in the third test in Sydney, they held firm. Once more, as in that famous victory, Johnson scored a try at a critical moment which Wood converted to stretch the lead back to eight points. Try as they might the home team could not breach the British defence until the very last minute when Wilson touched down and the successful conversion reduced the lead to three points. The final score was New Zealand 13 points Northern Union 16 points.

Unfortunately, the diplomacy shown by Wagstaff in his after-match comments had not been replicated in Europe as Germany declared war on Russia at 5.15pm, German time. With France and Britain as signatories to a defence treaty with Russia a Europe wide war was now inevitable.

The news of war had not yet reached the New Zealand papers so that evening the victorious British side were celebrating another victory. Since losing their first two games the tourists had recorded an impressive thirteen wins with their only defeat coming in the second test.

Harold Wagstaff and John Clifford sat in the hotel lounge after dinner to have their, now regular, review of the game.

'It's a bit strange doing the review without Joe isn't it?' Harold started the conversation.

'Yes, it does seem a bit odd but with all the bother in Europe our travel arrangements must come first. He was disappointed that he couldn't see the Test match, but as I said, Harold, it was a question of priorities.'

'Aye right enough, let's hope he can sort something out on the travel front. I take it the offer of two more test matches wasn't taken up then?'

'No, the unrest in Europe put paid to that idea too. Any road let's get down to business, what did you make of today's game then Harold?'

'It was a tough one, like I said to the press after the game. I think with us having such a good start we all thought it was going to be easy and maybe we dropped our intensity a bit. Once the New Zealanders got back into the game the momentum was with them. In the end we were hanging on a bit. But I always thought our defence would be strong enough to hold them out. Still, I was very relieved when Chick scored that try.'

'I think that's a very fair assessment Harold. We've been on a good run, and we've put some fine performances together here in New Zealand. Happen we did ease off a bit after getting those three tries. But those New Zealanders just seemed to roll their sleeves up and get stuck in, just when we expected them to roll over. If we play like that against the cream of New South Wales, we could find ourselves getting beaten.'

'We've got nigh on two weeks before that final game but a fair chunk of that will be on board the ship. We'll have a natter with all the boys while we're sailing and then we'll get some hard work in on the training pitch when we get to Melbourne.'

'Fair enough Harold. We'll be picking Joe up in Sydney so we can have another chat once he's on board. Now you can join the lads and have a bit of a celebration on a job well done.'

With the next game nearly two weeks away the players were able to let their hair down for a change, however the cloud of war was hovering over them. The main topic of conversation in Auckland was the prospect of a European war. The players had pushed it to the backs of their minds as their focus was on the preparation for the test match against New Zealand. Now that the game was out of the way they started to chat about the implications for them on the other side of the world.

Billie Jarman, Walter Romans and Jack Robinson had special reason to be concerned, they were all reservists and, as such, were required to report to their regiment within 24 hours in the event of war being declared. What would they be expected to do now that war had been declared whilst they were on the other side of the world?

The team would have a short stop-over in Sydney on their way to the final match of the tour in Melbourne. On arrival in Sydney the trio of reservists made their way to the British Embassy and there they were informed that they should report to their regiments within 24 hours of their arrival in England. At this point in time nobody was sure just when that would be.

Saturday 15th August, Melbourne

By the time the touring party reached Melbourne Britain had, as expected, joined the war.

In Melbourne, the state capital of Victoria, Australian Rules football was the number one sport. The New South Wales Rugby League had been having discussions with the league in Melbourne about the possibility of somehow merging the two games to create an Australia wide sport which would allow inter-state games between the two states as well as Queensland. This 'exhibition' game was seen as a step towards the potential amalgamation.

So on a breezy day, a crowd of around 20,000 inquisitive sports fans assembled at the famous Melbourne Cricket Ground to watch the first ever football match under Northern Union rules played in the state of Victoria. The team selected to represent New South Wales included a number of new faces. Sid Deane, who had captained Australia in the test matches, was already on his way to join his new team, Hull, in England and several of the other Sydney based players declined to travel.

The tourists fielded a strong team for the final match in Australia before heading home. The backs lined up Wood, Moorhouse, Wagstaff, Jenkins, Davies, Hall and Rogers. Chilcott, Ramsdale, Coldrick, Clampitt, Johnson and Longstaff made up the forwards.

The New South Wales team's new faces were Challis at full back, Leggo on the wing, Cubitt at half back and in the forwards Williams, Courtney and the Burge brothers.

Despite the fact that the match in Melbourne was promoted as an exhibition match between England and Australia there was nothing friendly about the proceedings, as the sides went at each other like demons. Most of the spectators were unfamiliar with the Northern Union rules but appreciated the handling skills and fast flowing moves of both sides in what turned out to be a closely fought game. The scrums seemed to cause great hilarity amongst the onlookers as the two packs of forwards pushed and shoved – and even appeared to kick – each other to try to win the ball.

Not for the first time in games on tour the Northern Union played the majority of the game one man short, although an injury to one of their players wasn't the problem this time. The scrums had become a real battle ground and eventually one erupted as an Australian forward kicked his opposite number before landing a couple of blows with his fists. Fortunately, for the guilty party, the referee was on the other side of the scrum and did not see the incident. This must have riled the visitors pack even more and shortly afterwards Fred Longstaff decided to take the law into his own hands resulting in him being ordered from the field for rough play. Not surprisingly the decision did not go down well with Longstaff's colleagues who protested to the referee.

The game itself mirrored the previous game against Auckland, as the tourists built up an early lead only to be pulled back by an opposition rally. A Jenkins try and three goals from Alf Wood gave them a nine-point lead before Pearce and Tidyman scored tries with one converted by A B Burge. The score was 9 points to 8 in favour of the tourists when Longstaff received his marching orders and remained so until half time.

The game continued to provide excellent entertainment for the spectators as the lead would change hands four times in the second half. Burge was the first to score as he landed another goal for the home team to take the lead for the first time, only for Wood to cancel it out with two of his own, 13 – 10 to the tourists. Halloway then scored for the home team and Burge landed the conversion to make it 15 – 13 in their favour. Shortly afterwards Wood landed another goal to level the scores. Once again, the character of the tourists was being tested to the full, but the twelve men found a way to win as Coldrick and then Moorhouse registered late tries to take them to a deserved 21 points to 15 victory. The second half had been fiercely contested resulting in Leggo for the home side and Chilcott for the tourists suffering serious head injuries with both players having to leave the field.

Longstaff's sending off was not the only incident which occurred and was highlighted by the press. At the start of the second half the home team entered the field along with the referee and touch judges, but the tourists did not. Eventually a touch judge was sent to the dressing room and in due course the touring team did appear, led by Wagstaff, to a round of applause. The newspapers later speculated that the team had initially refused to reappear unless Longstaff was reinstated to the team although this was never confirmed or denied by the touring team.

So, the experiment of playing a game in Melbourne under Northern Union rules was considered a success. The attendance of around 18,000, no doubt, benefitted from all local games being cancelled that day to allow the players and fans to attend the game. The crowd had been entertained by some free-flowing passing and combinations although the standard of the game was not quite as high as in the test series. The New South Wales league reported a loss on the game as the tourists received a 65% share of the gate, meaning the New South

Wales share did not cover the high costs of transporting and accommodating the Sydney based players.

Joe Houghton had booked the squad on that evening's sailing on board the RMS Orantes for London, so there was very little time for celebration in Melbourne.

As the ship sailed out of the harbour in Melbourne Joe Houghton approached Harold Wagstaff as they both waved to the well-wishers on shore. 'Just what went on at half time then, Harold?'

'It was summat and nowt Joe. We were all a bit annoyed at Fred getting sent off and the Aussie staying on. One of the lads, I forget who it was, said we ought to get him re-instated and a few others agreed. I just had to remind them about the clause in our contracts about sportsmanship, and then I pointed out that throughout the tour we had played by the rules, even the ones we didn't agree with.'

'You mean the replacement rule don't you.'

'Aye that's the one. Anyway, I said we should go out there and win the game for Fred and the lads all agreed. That's when the linesman came in, I didn't realise we were late coming out until then.'

'So, who was this mystery man who suggested we insisted on Fred being reinstated, Harold?'

Harold smiled 'I really can't remember Joe.'

Joe Houghton gave Harold Wagstaff a quizzical look, but Harold's expression gave nothing away. 'Ever the diplomat Harold. They could do with somebody like you working at the Foreign Office!'

'Aye they don't seem to be making much of a go of it at the minute do they. 'Appen they need some new blood, but they can't have me Joe. I'm a dedicated Northern Union man. If I worked for the Foreign Office I'd have to play that other game, the one the toffs all play.'

'You wouldn't by any chance be referring to *Rugby Union* old man, would you?' Joe Houghton put on a posh accent. 'I certainly am old fellow' Harold joined in the parody. At this point John Clifford joined them 'What's going on here then with all the posh accents?' A question which clearly amused the other two.

Joe Houghton eventually collected himself. 'Sorry about that John, Harold was thinking of joining the Foreign Office as a diplomat. I was just giving him some coaching on how to speak.'

'Take no notice John' Harold interrupted, 'I've no desire to join that lot. Where have you been anyway, you're normally on deck with your good lady when we leave port.'

'My good lady, as you refer to her Harold, is a trifle indisposed. I was just settling her down in our cabin. Have I missed anything?'

'I was just asking Harold about them being late out for the second half, turns out it was a storm in a tea-cup after all. I'll fill you in later John.'

John Clifford turned to address Harold. 'Fine win today Harold. The second half performance was very err,' he struggled to find the right word 'gritty. Yes, that's the word, the lads really had to grind out that win. What was Fred Longstaff sent off for anyway, I didn't see anything myself.'

'Did you see the incident a few minutes earlier when the Aussie started throwing punches in the scrum?'

'Aye I did, dirty bugger. I think the only person who didn't see it was the referee actually.'

'Well Fred was on the receiving end of a kick and a couple of punches and' it was Harold's turn to pause as he chose his words carefully. 'Let's just say he decided to get his own back, only this time the ref saw it.'

'Oh, well I suppose he had to go then, he should have known better and done it on the sly. We haven't had the best of luck with the referees over here have we? I was right pleased that we kept our unbeaten run going though. Listen you two, I'd better get back and check on the missus. Let's have a full review tomorrow morning after breakfast.'

'That's a good idea John, let's say about 10 o'clock, is that alright with you Harold?'

'Yes, that'll be fine for me. I'm going to catch up with some of the lads now, I'll see you two in the morning then.'

CHAPTER 19 – THE JOURNEY HOME

Sunday 16th August, on board RMS Orontes

'Well gentlemen I think the powers that be at the Northern Union will be well satisfied with the tour. The New South Wales League have informed me that our share of the gate receipts will amount to over £7,500[19]. Then there's the receipts from the Queensland and New Zealand games to add on top of the that[20]. And that should put a smile on the players faces, they will be in line for a nice bonus.' No wonder Joe Houghton was smiling. The tour had been a commercial success with receipts well in excess of expectations and considerably higher than on the previous tour in 1910.

'Well the lads will be right pleased to hear that Joe. Any idea how much it will be?' asked Harold.

'We'll have to wait for the accountants to do the detailed sums, but it will be a pretty penny for sure. I believe Jimmy Lomas and the squad got £30 each for the 1910 tour.'

'How does our playing record compare with the 1910 tourists then Joe?'

'You're in an inquisitive mood today aren't you Harold? Now, bearing in mind that the two tours didn't have exactly the same itineraries, the latest tour's record compares very favourably with the previous one. In

1910 they lost four and drew one of their 18 games, whereas on this tour there were only the three losses. Interestingly enough, both squads lost their first two games in Sydney.'

The tourists returned to Britain on the Orient Lines cruiser RMS Orontes. It was later requisitioned by the Royal Navy and became a troup carrier. (Source Wikipedia).

'The press over here are always drawing a comparison between us and Jimmy Lomas's team. They were quite damning about us after those first two defeats weren't they.' Harold continued. 'But we've come a long way since then. I always said we'd be fine once we'd got the sea out of our legs and had some time together to sharpen our combinations.'

John Clifford supported Harold 'You did indeed Harold. None of the papers gave us much of a chance in the test matches after those two defeats. The way we walloped them in the first test certainly made them eat their words. I'm sure we'd have won the second one if Jack Robinson hadn't picked up that injury at the start of the second half.'

'You might well be right there, John' Harold responded. 'But it's kind of strange when you look back though. If we had won that second test the Ashes would have been ours and we wouldn't have had to win the third test in the way that we did.'

'I suppose when you look at it like that' Joe Houghton

was scratching his chin again as he thought long and hard about what to say. 'You could say the Aussies did us a favour winning that second test, AND the New South Wales League making us play like they did. Well it all worked out for the best in the end didn't it? I'll never forget, as long as I live, the feeling when Tom McMahon finally blew his whistle and the cheer that the crowd gave us. It was the best feeling I've ever had at the end of a game.'

'I think it was John's speech to the lads before the game that swung it our way. The look on the players faces, the absolute determination to win...' Harold paused to collect himself as he was in danger of being overcome by emotion. 'What was it you said, John? *You will win as it is right versus wrong* or something like that?'

'I can't remember my exact words, but it was something like that. I hadn't prepared a speech y'know, the words just came from my heart' it was now John Clifford's turn to let his emotions show.

'Oh, stop your blubbering or you'll have me at it in a minute.' Joe Houghton's sharp words brought them back to reality. 'The issue about the New South Wales league changing the fixture and sending the cable hasn't finished yet though. John and I will be taking it up with the Northern Union Management Committee when we get back won't we John?'

'Aye, we certainly will, and I shall be standing by my commitment to resign in principle about the matter.'

Harold tried to dissuade him 'Don't be hasty John, you've got nigh on another six weeks before we get back home, you might see things differently then.'

'Wise words Harold' Joe Houghton backed him up and looked at John Clifford.

Clifford simply crossed his arms and muttered 'We'll see.'

The first stage of the journey involved sailing along the south coast of Australia from Melbourne to Freemantle. Problems with enemy ships weren't expected in these southerly waters. To everyone's surprise, when they arrived in Freemantle, it was reported that a German vessel had been seen in the area. The next stage of the journey would take them north to Colombo, where the Orontes would be in much greater danger from German war ships. Therefore, the captain was advised to sail at night without lights to avoid detection by any enemy vessels which may be in the area. To everyone's relief the Orontes did arrive in Colombo safely and without incidents. Protection was waiting for them at Colombo; and from that point onwards they were escorted, on both sides, by Royal Navy cruisers all the way through the Red Sea, the Suez Canal and across the Mediterranean. The final section of the journey would be the most perilous as they made their way north past the Portuguese coastline and the Bay of Biscay before heading for the safety of their homeland.

For the battered and bruised players, the first part of the journey presented them with the opportunity to rest their weary bodies and relax.

After a few days lounging around Harold started to look forward to the next season of Northern Union rugby. As he leaned on the railing at the front of the boat with his fair hair flapping in the wind his mind began to wander. What would the season hold, would there actually be a league competition in view of the war? What had gone wrong for him and his talented team at the end of the previous season which had promised so much but, in the end, fizzled out in disappointment and defeat in the two major competitions? During the tour he had put his frustrations on one side to focus exclusively on the tour and the objective of bringing back the Ashes.

His daydreaming was interrupted by his great pal, Douglas Clark who strode up to him and slapped him on his back. 'A penny for them 'Arold.'

'Oh, it's you Duggie, I was miles away.'

'Yes, I could see that. What's troubling the great master today then 'Arold?'

'Tell the truth Duggie I was thinking about the next season when we get back to Yorkshire.'

'That's just typical of you 'Arold. Here we are sailing along the south coast of Australia and your minds on the other side of the world planning our next campaign.'

'You know me too well Duggie. It's just, y'know, we've come over here to get the Ashes and, well we've done it haven't we. I suppose you could say I'm a restless soul, I need another goal to aim for.'

'Oh come on 'Arold. You've won every honour a man can in the Northern Union. You've got winners medals for every cup and league competition. Captain of your club, Yorkshire and now you've captained the team that won the Ashes. What more is there to go for?'

'I suppose all that's true Duggie, but the way last season finished up is still bothering me. We had the Yorkshire Cup and League in the bag, finished top of the league table and were in with a chance in the two big competitions. I really thought we could emulate what Hunslet did a few years back and win all four trophies in the same season.'

'Aye lad, I think we all thought that. 'Appen that's why we missed out on the big two, losing to Hull and then Salford. No disrespect to either of 'em, they're both good teams, but we should have beaten them both.'

'The papers reckoned it was 'cos we were all saving ourselves for the tour. Y'know, didn't want to get injured like and miss the boat. At the time I thought it was rubbish, but now...' he paused. 'Now I'm not so sure.'

'I'm damn sure we all did our best, but maybe, just maybe, at the back of our minds the possibility...' Douglas Clark didn't finish his sentence, but Harold Wagstaff got the message.

'Duggie, if we want, really want' he placed extra emphasis on the word really, 'Huddersfield to go down as a truly great side we have to match what Hunslet did and win all four. This coming season has to be the one. That's if there is a league this season.'

'But we don't get back while the end of September, there'll be four or five games gone before we even land.'

'True enough Duggie. Let's hope the lads back home can get a few wins in before we join them. Once we get into the med, we need to step up our training to make sure we're fully fit when we get back home. Will you be ready to start training again by then?'

'Well the shoulder's starting to feel a bit better now 'Arold. The doctor said to rest it until the middle of September and then build it back up slowly. To be honest it's touch and go if I'll be fit by the time we get home, but I'm going to give it my best shot.'

'I'm sure you will Duggie, but there's no point rushing back before you're ready and then getting injured again, like I did back in 1910. Anyway, we don't even know if the Northern Union will be running a league competition this year, with the war and all that stuff going on.'

'Even if there is a league, we're going to be facing a lot of competition this year 'Arold. I see your mate Sid Deane is lakin' for Hull this time and they already had a decent side with Gilbert and Batten and a few others. I hear they're paying him a small fortune, aren't they?'

'He's a damn good laker is Snowy, he'd be an asset to any team. Mind you I don't believe all this stuff in the papers about how much he's getting.'

'I reckon Wigan will be challenging for the title as well. It's going to feel really strange playing against lads like Bert Jenkins when we've been team-mates supporting each other in some tight corners won't it?'

'You're not wrong there Duggie, it is going to be weird. But it'll be the same for them won't it.'

Douglas Clark smiled at the prospect of lining up against his tour companions. 'Come on 'Arold, that's enough deep thinking for one day, let's do a couple of rounds of the deck and get that stiffness out and build up an appetite for luncheon.' So, the two friends set off to do a tour of the deck, not that they got very far as they kept bumping into small groups of team-mates every fifty yards or so where they would stop to have a chat.

CHAPTER 20 – THE HOMECOMING

The RMS Orontes duly arrived at Plymouth on the 26th September 1914. This was two days earlier than the draft schedule, as the original itinerary included a stop at Naples which had to be cancelled due to the war arrangements. Officials from the Northern Union were there to greet the victorious team, but there were no great crowds assembled to celebrate their achievements and give them the hero's welcome they deserved. Plymouth was an important naval port and, not surprisingly, most people's attention was drawn to the war.

By the time that the tourists reached home shores major battles on both the Eastern and Western Fronts had taken place. On the Eastern Front the German army had twice defeated the Russian army at the battles of Tannenberg and Masurian Lakes inflicting great losses on the Russian side. Whilst on the Western Front the first battle of the Marne had taken place where the French, with the help of the British forces, had managed to stop the German advance on Paris and had counter attacked themselves. Both sides then 'dug in' and the trench warfare which was to become a feature of the war and cost so many lives on both sides had begun.

All the players, with the possible exception of the three reservists, were keen to find out if the Northern Union was running a league competition. They were told by the officials that, after careful consideration of all the facts, the league had decided that the games would take place as normal.

When Harold enquired as to the fortunes of his Huddersfield team, he was told that they had won just two of their four games so far, having lost one and drawn one. Another game, against York, was taking place that day but the result was not known.

Harold turned to one of his Huddersfield colleagues 'Did you hear that Johnny, we've played four won two, lost one and drawn one.'

'Not so good then 'Arold.'

'Aye, but it's only to be expected considering half the team aren't there isn't it' he replied.

'Well at least the reinforcements are coming' Johnny Rogers joked.

The touring party travelled together by train as far as London where the Lancashire and Yorkshire contingents shook hands and said farewell before making the final stage of their journey home, on their respective train lines.

When John Clifford, Harold Wagstaff and the rest of the Huddersfield representatives finally arrived at their home station the reporter from the Huddersfield Examiner was waiting to greet them. Before the reporter had time to ask them for comments Harold shot out a question of his own. 'How have the lads done today?'

'They've drawn 7 points all with York actually.'

'Oh crikey, another point dropped lads. Let's see that six points from five games.' Harold looked disappointed.

'Don't worry 'Arold, remember the reinforcements have arrived' Johnny Rogers repeated his joke of earlier, and to emphasise the point put his hand to his mouth, rolling his fingers together and made the sound of a bugle. The rest of his team-mates enjoyed the joke and broke out in laughter, even Harold had to smile.

'Yes, well the reinforcements had better do a good job. We can't afford to drop many more points. I want to see you all at training this week, and no shirking.'

'Oh give us a break 'Arold we've only just got back' chimed Stan Moorhouse.

'Give us a break? You've just spent 6 weeks sunning yourself on deck you idle buggers.'

Douglas Clark put his arm around his captain's shoulders 'Take not notice of them 'Arold, the lads are only having a bit of fun. You know we'll all be there giving it our all.'

CHAPTER 21 – A RECORD-BREAKING SEASON

Monday 28th September, Holmfirth

After a well earned lie in on Sunday Harold was up bright and early and made his way into the village of Holmfirth to pick up a morning paper. It was a bright sunny day so, after collecting his paper, he made his way across the road to the bridge over the River Holme where he paused to lean on the stone wall.

The front page of his Daily Mirror was dominated by news from the war front. He gave it a cursory glance and sighed before turning to the back pages where the sports news would be found. Association Football was already the dominant sport and covered the back page, so he flicked back a page or two until he found the section on Northern Union. He quickly found the section with the league tables where he found his Huddersfield team were lying in mid-table. 'Not surprising' he thought to himself, 'with six points from five games it's only to be expected'. He did some mental arithmetic 'There's 34 games in a season so we've still got 29 to go. We finished top last year with 58 points so, we need to pick up 52 points from our remaining games to match last season.

It's going to be tough, but we can do it. We had a bad start to the tour but once we got going, we didn't do too bad.' A smile returned to the young man's face. 'Yes, we can do it, we will do it.'

A look of grim determination was set on his face as he walked into the family home where his father was sat at the kitchen table smoking his pipe. 'We CAN do it Father I know we can.'

'You can do what son?'

'We can still win the league. Now that we're all back from Australia we can go on a run and put some points on the board.'

'Of course you can lad, there's still 30 games to go, the season's only just started.'

'It's 29 actually father, but you're right. I can't wait to get back on that pitch at Fartown. I tell you what I'm going to start now by getting my shorts on and going for a run before breakfast.'

'Ee lad, your firm has given you a couple of days off to rest after the journey. Can't you just relax?'

'I don't need the rest father, I need to be fit and ready to play. A run will do me good, get all that travelling out of my system. And I'll be back at work tomorrow, I can't do with sitting around.'

Andrew Wagstaff knew there was no point protesting. When it came to rugby matters the lad could be very stubborn.

Saturday 3rd October, Fartown, Huddersfield

Douglas Clark was given another week to recover from his injury and Fred Longstaff also missed out on a place in the team. The other four tourists, Wagstaff, Moorhouse, Rogers and Chilcott were all in the team selected to meet Batley. All four of the returning players were looking rusty but the team managed to grind out a 10 points to 5 win against a plucky Batley side. Albert Rosenfeld had started the season well and his two tries in this game took his season's tally to eight and Ben Gronow added two goals.

In the changing room after the match, Harold Wagstaff was typically blunt in his assessment of the team's performance. 'That was bloody hard work lads. We really had to dig deep to get the win, but if we lake like that next week at Barrow we'll come back empty handed.'

Wagstaff and Johnny Rogers were the last to leave the changing rooms. Johnny was putting his coat on and Harold was tying his shoelaces when Johnny broke the silence. 'Looks like our reinforcements were firing blanks today 'Arold.'

Harold stern expression cracked into a smile, 'You can say that again. I don't know about you Johnny but I was struggling a bit out there. I suppose that's what six weeks at sea does for you.'

'I was just the same 'Arold. Before the game I felt really good and confident, but my timing was off and there were times when I was blowing out of my backside. Still we've got another week now to acclimatise before we travel up to Cumberland. I bet Dougie Clark will want to play next week as it's old stamping ground isn't it.'

'Yeh, when I spoke to him last night, he was determined to be fit for that one. Hopefully Fred will be back as well.'

10ᵗʰ October, Barrow-in-Furness

The journey back from Barrow was long and miserable one for the Huddersfield team. With all six of their tourists back in the team they were expected to be too strong for a Barrow team who had finished just outside the play off positions in the previous season.

Another lack lustre display by Huddersfield fulfilled Wagstaff's prediction and they were duly beaten by 18 points to 8, with Wagstaff and Moorhouse each scoring a try and Ben Gronow a goal. Wagstaff cut a dejected figure as he made his way home.

Andrew Wagstaff didn't need to ask him how the team had got on, defeat was written all over his son's face.

'If we carry on playing like that father, we won't win a thing this time, and I had such high hopes.'

Andrew Wagstaff wasn't going to let his son mope over the result of a rugby match. 'Pull yersen together lad, you've lost a game of rugby. There's lads your age out there in France losing their lives, what have you got to complain about?'

His father's words hit Harold like a hammer, and he was stunned. After a moment or two he collected himself. 'You're dead right father. I haven't got anything to moan about have I. I've just been half-way around the world, all expenses paid. I've been introduced to Prime Ministers and MP's and Mayors by the dozen. What have I got to complain about?' He jumped up off his chair and ran over to his father and gave him a tremendous hug. 'Thanks father, that kick up the backside was just what I needed. Rugby is important – but it's not life or death.' And with that he took himself off to bed with a smile on his face.

Andrew Wagstaff sat back down in his chair, lit his pipe and drew heavily on it. As he blew the smoke out in a cloud, he smiled and muttered 'Well I'll be blowed.'

Huddersfield's next game would be a Yorkshire Cup Tie at York, never an easy place to win, in fact they had scraped a 7 points all draw only two weeks earlier in the league. Huddersfield had a great record in the Yorkshire Cup having won the cup the previous season and three times in the last five seasons. It was to be a turning point in Huddersfield's stop-start season as the victory they achieved was the start of an unbeaten run of 13 games up to the end of the year.

On 28th November the Yorkshire Cup Final took place and Huddersfield faced Hull at Headingley. Hull had knocked the high flying Huddersfield team out of the Challenge Cup at the semi final stage in the previous season and were a formidable team that included Billy Batten and were captained by the famous Australian Bert Gilbert. Also included in their line-up was Harold's friend and rival captain from the Ashes series Sid Deane. A close contest was expected, with Hull as slight favourites.

Wagstaff's team had started to play with the fluency for which they had become famous and had produced a fourteen try demolition of the once mighty Hunslet in the semi-final, with Wagstaff and Moorhouse each scoring four tries. In the changing rooms before the match Harold rallied his troops. 'Right lads, this lot turned us over in the Challenge Cup semi-final last year, so we owe them one. They were a good side last year and they've now got Snowy Deane in the centres and we know a bit about Snowy, don't we lads?'

'Aye 'Arold we should do. We played against him five times over there' Stan Moorhouse supported his captain.

'It's up to us lads. If we play to our ability, we will beat any side, so let's go out there and show them what we're made of.' The rallying cry had the desired effect and generated a cheer from the players as they all stood up and, with determination etched on their faces, marched out of the changing room and into the tunnel where the Hull team were already assembled.

Harold shook hands with his old friend Snowy Deane, but no words were spoken as the two teams made their way out onto the Headingley pitch to be welcomed by the roar of the crowd.

The expected close encounter didn't materialise as Wagstaff's team brushed Hull aside and ran in seven tries in a 31 points to nil victory. Wagstaff led the way with two tries as Huddersfield retained the Yorkshire Cup.

The two teams were to meet again at Huddersfield on Christmas day, and Huddersfield once more came out on top, however the contest was much closer with the final score 20 points to 10 in their favour. The game was remarkable as it was played on the cricket pitch at the side of the normal rugby field.

Huddersfield finished the year off with a convincing 44 points to 4 victory away at Wakefield. Stan Moorhouse being the destroyer in chief as he ran in four of his sides ten tries.

January was a busy period for the Fartowners as they packed seven straight wins into the month. Most were by comfortable margins apart from the home match with Wigan which they won by the narrowest of margins, 7 points to 6. Their final game in January came on the 30th when they hammered Bramley by 79 points to nil with the wingers, Rosenfeld and Moorhouse scoring six tries each out of the overall total of nineteen.

Huddersfield's wonderful winning run of 26 games came to an end on 20th February when they were held to a 5 points all draw at Leeds, who, along with Wigan, were emerging as Huddersfield's main challengers at the top of the league.

Huddersfield had another close win the week after this when they beat Leigh by 3 points to nil in the Challenge

Cup. Another draw followed a week later, this time it was Hull Kingston Rovers who held Huddersfield to 15 points all.

It was back to winning ways the following week as Widnes were despatched by 29 points to 3 on their own territory in the Challenge Cup.

There was no stopping the Fartowners from this point as they won their final six league matches with an aggregate score of 221 points against 58. In their final league match they defeated York by 30 points to 11. Huddersfield's unbeaten record since the defeat at Barrow on 10th October was played 30, won 28, drawn 2. During this period, they had also won 4 Yorkshire Cup Ties and 3 Challenge Cup Ties. They had, therefore, already collected the Yorkshire League and Cup trophies and were now in the semi-finals of both the Challenge Cup and the League Championship play offs. Wagstaff's team stood on threshold of greatness. Four more wins from the two semi-finals and then two finals would enable them to emulate the great Hunslet side who had won all four trophies in one season back in 1908.

They had just played and won three games in four days and now had just four days to prepare to meet the mighty Wigan in the Challenge Cup semi-final at Parkside, the home of Hunslet, whilst Rochdale Hornets awaited them in the play-off semi-final a week later.

Saturday 10th April 1914, Hunslet, Leeds

As the Huddersfield players assembled in the changing rooms Douglas Clark turned to Harold Wagstaff 'Four games in eight days 'Arold. Does it take you back to that day in Sydney?'

'Aye it does that, I just hope we don't run into a load of injuries today Duggie, how about you?'

As well as being a rugby international, Douglas Clark was a top class wrestler. Like most players he also had a 'day job' as a coalman. (Courtesy Huddersfield RL Heritage)

'Aye it does that, I just hope we don't run into a load of injuries today Duggie, how about you?'

'Talk about highs and lows 'Arold. When I left that pitch in Sydney for the final time it felt like the lowest point of my career. I could see all that we'd worked for disappearing. Down to eleven men against the pride of Australia. I really thought we'd had it, but I didn't reckon on you lads holding out like you did. When that whistle blew it was the highest point of my career, the relief I felt was enormous. All the pain vanished into thin air; I was so proud of you all.'

'Aye it was a wonderful moment I'll give you that. D'you know the thing that sticks in my mind the most is the way the crowd cheered us that day and the reception they gave us at the end. It brings a tear to my eye even now when I think back.' He paused and regained his composure. 'Any road it's another day today, another challenge. Once we've all got changed, I want to say a few words.'

A few minutes later, when the whole team were sat in their playing strip Harold rose to his feet. 'We've come a long way together this season lads. From a mediocre start, when everybody was writing us off, we've got our heads down and put together a fantastic run. Everybody has us down as favourites to win today but cast your mind back twelve months to when we faced Salford in the final. We were odds on that day lads, but we still finished up beaten. Just think back to how it felt that day when we came off that pitch defeated. Wigan are a good side and we'll need to be at our best to beat them. We have the talent now let's go out there and show the world what this Huddersfield team can do.'

Wagstaff needn't have worried as his Huddersfield team didn't let him down as they simply brushed aside Wigan by 27 points to 2. Albert Rosenfeld scored 4 tries, Johnny Rogers bagged a brace and Stan Moorhouse also scored. Ben Gronow landed three goals.

As the victorious team gathered in the changing room Harold congratulated them all 'Well done lads, that was the performance I wanted. That's one down and three to go. Rochdale next week and I'll be looking for a repeat of today's effort'. He made his way over to Albert Rosenfeld and patted him on the shoulder 'Well played Rozzy.'

'Cheers 'Arold' came the reply. Albert Rosenfeld had developed a real Yorkshire twang to go with his Aussie accent. 'You lads in the centre make it easy for me and Stan on the wing. Isn't that right Stan?'

'Aye Rozzy, piece of cake.'

'Well I wish you wingers would make it a bit easier for me with the goal kicks' Ben Gronow chimed in. 'Can you try and get a bit closer to the posts next week lads?' A chorus of laughter came up from the rest of the players.

Douglas Clark turned to his captain and, in a low tone of voice said 'There's nothing to compare with a winning dressing room is there 'Arold?'

'You can say that again Duggie. Losing stinks.'

Saturday 17ᵗʰ April 1914, Fartown, Huddersfield

By virtue of finishing top of the league Huddersfield would have home advantage in the play-off semi-final against Rochdale Hornets who finished fourth in the league. Wigan had finished runners up to Huddersfield and therefor had the privilege of a home fixture against the third placed team, Leeds.

Huddersfield carried on from where they left off the previous week and delivered a resounding 33 points to 2 victory over their rivals from the other side of the Pennines. Albert Rosenfeld went one better that the previous week by notching five of Huddersfield's seven tries, the other try scorers being Stan Moorhouse and Tommy Gleeson. Ben Gronow landed six goals. In the other semi-final Leeds upset the odds by defeating Wigan by 15 points to 4 to qualify to meet Huddersfield in the final.

The Huddersfield changing room was a happy place to be as they celebrated victory. Rozzy had been in electrifying form and was understandably jubilant at scoring five tries in such an important game. He called out to Ben Gronow, the team's goal-kicker, 'How was that Ben, did I get close enough to the posts for you this week?'

'Yes thanks Rozzy that was a lot better. I'd like more of the same next week please.'

'Aye another five next week against Leeds will be just the job Albert' agreed Fred Longstaff.

Douglas Clark turned to his captain, 'Leeds must have played well today to win over at Wigan 'Arold, I wasn't expecting that.'

'No neither was I Duggie. Wigan's a tough place to go and get a win. My mate Bert Jenkins will be disappointed not to make the final, especially after we beat them in the Challenge Cup semi last week as well.'

'Just the two finals left now 'Arold. It's off to Belle Vue

next week and then Watersheddings the week after.'

'Aye well I'm not looking any further than Leeds next week for the Championship. We'll think about St Helens in the Cup Final once we've got that one out of the way.'

24th April 1914, Belle Vue, Wakefield

The Huddersfield team which made it's way the short distance to Wakefield was in confident mood for the Championship Final. And well they might be with convincing seven try victories against Wigan and Rochdale in the last two games. It wasn't just their attack that was performing well, their defence had not been penetrated as they had restricted their opponents to one goal in each of the semi-finals.

Huddersfield were able to field the same team for the third week in a row, so Harold Wagstaff kept his pre-match speech to a minimum. 'Alright lads, this is it, the championship final. I'm looking for another performance like the last two today. No slip ups – remember Salford. Now let's get out there and win it the Huddersfield way.'

Wagstaff wasn't disappointed, his team went out and, just as they had done in the previous two games, simply overwhelmed their opponents. For the third match in a row they registered seven tries. Ben Gronow put in a man of the match performance with two tries and seven goals in their 35 points to 2 victory. For once Albert Rosenfeld didn't get on the scoresheet as Wagstaff, Moorhouse, Rogers, Clark and Longstaff also touched down.

As the victorious Huddersfield team made their way around the Belle Vue pitch on their lap of honour they saluted their supporters who had made the short trip across West Yorkshire to witness their success.

Over the last three matches the Fartowners had demonstrated their superiority by beating their three nearest challengers by an aggregate score of 95 points to 6. Only St Helens, who had finished the season in seventh place, stood between them and the cherished goal of 'All Four' trophies.

Back in the changing room the mood was buoyant. Albert Rosenfeld was congratulating Ben Gronow on his two tries and seven goals. 'Decided to score them yourself heh Ben that way you can make sure you manage the conversions.'

Ben replied in his thick Welsh accent 'Well I thought it was about time someone else got some glory. We've been letting you wingers get all the credit all season, now it's the forwards turn. What d'you forwards think?'

Fred Longstaff was the first to react, 'That's right Ben, us lads in the pack have been making it easy for you backs all season, it's our turn now.'

The celebrations went on as the players jumped into the communal bath. Harold Wagstaff, who had been doing his after the match interviews with the press, was the last to arrive and was unceremoniously dumped into the water still wearing his playing kit by his jubilant colleagues. A bottle of champagne appeared from somewhere, was emptied into the Championship trophy and passed around the players.

A few days later a civic reception took place and the crowds gathered outside the Town Hall to cheer their conquering heroes. As the players enjoyed the applause of their faithful fans John Clifford approached Harold Wagstaff. 'It's been quite a year for you Harold. Bringing back the Ashes and now securing the Championship and the Cup Final still to come. So why are you looking so serious?'

'Sorry John, I was just thinking about St Helens on Saturday. You know me I'm always looking forward to the next challenge.'

'Can't you just enjoy the moment like the rest of the lads?'

'I suppose I should but....' His voiced tailed off and he gave a big sigh. 'What I really want is for this Huddersfield side to go down in history as one of the greatest.'

'Oh, I think that's already been achieved, look at our record over the last few years.'

'That might be the case, at the moment John. But to be remembered in years to come we need to do something extra special, like Hunslet did a few years ago. We need to win all four, simple as that. That's why I'm thinking about St Helens on Saturday, we've just got to beat them. Chances are, with the way the war is shaping up, there won't be a proper league next season, and who knows when the war'll be over, so it's now or never.'

'The way the lads are playing I have every confidence that you'll complete the job on Saturday and take your rightful place in rugby history.'

Brave words from John Clifford but Harold was still not happy. 'Aye – confident! That's what we were last year against Salford and look what happened then. That match still haunts me, to this day and probably will till my dying day.'

'St Helens are a different proposition Harold. That Salford team had the best defence the Northern Union has ever seen. I know that everyone was saying that we couldn't lose and maybe – just maybe – the lads were a bit complacent, what with the tour coming up as well.'

'St Helens are a decent side John, you don't get to the final by being a poor side do you? If we go to Oldham with the wrong attitude, we could be in for another shock defeat.'

'Well we'd better make sure that the attitude is spot on then hadn't we? We need to keep them focussed all week, but let them enjoy themselves tonight, and you can show some leadership by joining in the fun as well.'

After the celebrations had finished Harold had a quiet word with Douglas Clark and they agreed to speak on a one to one basis with all the players before Saturday.

Saturday 1ˢᵗ May, Watersheddings, Oldham

The morning of the last game of the 1914-15 Northern Union season brought heavy rainfall which continued during the match. It must have brought a smile to the faces of the Saints players and fans who would be hoping that it would act as a great leveller and dull the ability of the Huddersfield team who, once more, were odds on favourites to seal their fourth trophy of the season.

Harold Wagstaff saw shades of their defeat by Salford in the championship final just a year ago. St Helens, like Salford, owed their progress to the final on a solid defence. They had made their way to the final by virtue of a 6 points to nil victory over Featherstone in round one, followed by a 5 nil win over Swinton in the second round. In the quarter final they had scraped through by the narrowest of margins by 3 points to 2 against Keighley. They were drawn against high flying Rochdale Hornets in the semi who they beat by 9 points to 2 in a replay after a five all draw in the first game. On their way to the final they had conceded only one try and three goals but had only scored a total of 28 points over the five games. Huddersfield, on the other hand, had amassed a total of 92 points and had only five points scored against them. Their first round game against Leigh had been a close one with

Huddersfield just edging it by three points to nil, but the other three games had seen convincing wins for the Fartowners as they despatched Widnes by 29 points to 3, Salford were trounced 33 nil and Wigan were brushed aside in the semi-final by 27 points to 2. Surely lightening couldn't strike twice and deny Huddersfield a place in history?

Clark and Wagstaff had been chatting with all the players in the week before the match so by the time the match came around Harold was confident that all his players were in the right frame of mind, totally focussed on the job in hand. He decided keep his pre-match chat brief, 'Right lads this is the moment. One more win today and you will all go down in history. This is our defining moment, give it everything you've got.' He even borrowed a line from the Northern Union's cable to the tourists before the third test match in Sydney, 'I want you to expend every atom of energy you have to win the cup for Huddersfield.'

Watersheddings, the home of the Oldham team, was certainly living up to its name as the kick-off time approached and the weather had affected the attendance with around 8,000 people present. St Helens won the toss and elected to play with the wind and rain behind them. Shortly after the game had started an unusual event occurred as the match ball burst. Was this an omen? The answer was emphatically no! Within three minutes Huddersfield had taken the lead with a fine try by Tommy Gleeson. Ben Gronow who had only taken over the goal-kicking from Major Holland in December started the match needing three more goals to equal the record set by Carmichael of Hull Kingston Rovers. He was unable to convert Gleeson's try but soon made amends as

Wagstaff and then Rosenfeld both scored tries which he converted to open up a 13 point lead for Huddersfield.

Ben Gronow went into the final match of the season needing just three goals to beat the record number of goals in a season. (Courtesy Huddersfield RL Heritage).

The St Helens forwards were putting up a brave fight even though their best forward, Heaton, was missing due to illness, but they had no answer to the speed and accuracy of the Huddersfield backs. Wagstaff added another try followed shortly by Gleeson's second. Gronow converted Gleeson's try to register his third successful kick and thus equal Carmichael's record of 138 goals in a season. At half-time the score was 21 points to nil in favour of Huddersfield.

To their credit the St Helens players did not give up and their forwards in particular continued to challenge their more illustrious counterparts. Major Holland did add another try shortly after the interval but St Helens dug in and kept the Fartowners scoreless for the next twenty minutes. Eventually the scoring resumed with a try by Moorhouse which Ben Gronow converted to become the outright goalkicking record holder. The crowd gave him a round of applause in recognition of the feat. Gronow then took matters in his own hands and scored a try himself which he also converted to take his season's tally to 140. The score had now risen to 34 points to nil and Rogers added another try under the posts which Gronow somehow managed to miss. Just when it appeared that St Helens would be 'nilled' Daniels popped up to score a try which was not converted, leaving the final score 37 points to 3 in favour of Huddersfield.

When the referee blew the whistle to signal the end of the game the normally unemotional Wagstaff held his arms aloft to salute his team's achievement, and then sank to his knees. After receiving the cup from Mr J H Smith the Acting Chairman of the Northern Union, the Huddersfield Captain was lifted onto the shoulders of his teammates' proudly holding the trophy aloft to the cheers of their *fans*.As the Huddersfield players made their way into the changing rooms Douglas Clark had his arm around the shoulders of his captain 'Well 'Arold, we've done it at last. This Huddersfield team WILL go down in the history books as one of the truly great teams and you' he paused to shake his captain. 'You, 'Arold Wagstaff will go down in history as the greatest captain of all time.'

A pink glow could be seen through the mud spattered face of the young Huddersfield captain. He turned to address his great friend. 'Douglas, football is a team game and I have had the privilege to captain the greatest team, full of talented and committed players. I am proud of you all and what we have achieved as a team.'

The two of them were the last to enter the dressing room where the celebrations had already started. Someone had brought a bottle of champagne which had been emptied into the cup and was being passed from player to player. Albert Rosenfeld was doing a dance whilst wearing the top of the cup as a hat which suddenly slipped from his head and hit the stone floor with a crash. The room went silent for a moment before Rozzy picked it up, examined it before announcing 'No damage done lads' to a cheer of relief from around the dressing room.

'You'd best put it down before you do some damage to it Rozzy' shouted Johnny Rogers, and a sheepish looking Albert Rosenfeld duly complied.

The victorious Huddersfield 'Team of All the Talents' proudly displaying the four trophies. (Courtesy Huddersfield RL Heritage)

As the celebrations continued Harold Wagstaff sat quietly and soaked in the atmosphere as he watched his teammates behaving like little boys; their joy at winning another trophy knew no bounds. He had a great sense of satisfaction at what they had achieved together along with an overwhelming sense of relief that they had finally done what they had been threatening to do for several years only to fail at the last hurdle. He knew in his heart that these teammates, everyone of them a great friend, would probably never come together again to play Northern Union rugby; the war in Europe would see to that.

A few days later, when the dust had settled from their historic victory Harold was enjoying a quiet pint with his brother Norman. Every so often a stranger would walk up to them, shake Harold's hand and complement him on the team's success.

After about the fifth time this happened Norman ribbed his younger brother, 'You're quite the celebrity now little brother, what does it feel like?'

Harold smiled as he replied 'It's a bit embarrassing Norman to tell the truth. I still think of mesen as an ordinary bloke. I just happen to be quite handy at playing football.'

'Ah there you go again, you're far too modest 'Arold. Everybody thinks you're a genius and you think you're a bit handy. You wouldn't be captain of the best team the Northern Union has ever produced never mind the captain who led his country to bring back the Ashes from the other side of the world.'

'Oh, gerron with you Norman, you'll have me blushing at this rate.'

Before Norman had chance to respond another admirer approached them and congratulated Harold on the team's success. It was a young lad about 15 years old who had sneaked into the pub without the landlord spotting him. 'I j-just wanted t-to ask you M-Mr Wagstaff how you became such a g-good player, like and, and w-what advice you could give me to become a good laker?'

'What position do you play young man?' asked Harold.

'I play c-centre just like you sir, err Mr Wagstaff and I play for Milnsbridge J-juniors.'

'How old are you? 15? 16?'

'I'm 15, nearly 16 sir.'

'Well the best advice I can give you, young man is to work hard at developing your fitness and skills and have confidence in your own ability. Watch as much football as you can, especially the professional game, and study what the best players do. Most of all enjoy your sport and play with a smile on your face.'

Harold had barely finished giving the young man some advice when the Landlord spotted him and shouted 'What are you doing in here, bugger off you little ruffian and stop bothering my customers.'

'Oh it's alright he's not bothering us at all, we're just having a chat about football aren't we...' Harold looked at the lad 'what's your name sonny?'

'It's N-Norman sir. Norman Wilkinson.'

'Well you'd better run along Norman' Harold rubbed the hair of his new friend. 'You're a bit young to be in a pub and the landlord could lose his licence if the police see you.' Norman Wilkinson hesitated for a moment, when the landlord lifted his right hand up to his left shoulder as if preparing to give the lad a swipe, he quickly made a bee line for the door.

The Landlord turned to the Wagstaff brothers 'I'm sorry about that little rascal coming in here and annoying you gents.'

'Oh, don't worry about it. The lad just wanted a few tips and I was happy to oblige' replied Harold.

'I can remember what you were up to when you were his age 'Arold. You were lakin' for Fartown weren't you. Just look at what you've achieved in, what will it be, eight years.'

'Like I said Norman, I've been lucky. I started with Fartown when they were struggling a bit but they went out and brought some good lakers in. Folk like Edgar Wrigley,

Con Byrne and Rozzy and a few more. From that point we were on the up and I've loved every minute of it.'

'Aye, you've had your fair share of triumphs and won a bagful of medals; but you've had a few downs as well haven't you. 1910 was a bad year for you, getting that injury which turned to blood poisoning and after that you went and got diphtheria. I remember how disappointed you were when you didn't get picked for the tour of Australia at the end of the season.'

'You're right Norman that was a real setback for me. I was very disappointed but, as I recall, you and Father told me my chance would come and you weren't wrong big brother. Credit where credit's due.'

'Well you haven't looked back since, and what a year you've just had. Ashes winner and then all four trophies. But it didn't look so good when you all got back from your travels did it?'

'No it didn't. Johnny Rogers said the team was waiting for the reinforcements to arrive. Not that we did any better at first. When we went up to Barrow and lost' Harold shook his head. 'I thought our chances had gone this year. But the lads got their heads down and we went on that run, and we haven't looked back since.'

'D'you reckon the war has had an impact 'Arold?'

'Oh, for sure Norman. Quite a few of our competitors have had players swapping their rugby jerseys for khaki. We've been lucky in that regard and have managed to keep the team pretty much together. I felt a bit sorry for St Helens last week, they've only had about 15 players to choose from and then they lost their best forward, Heaton through illness just before the final. They put up a good fight though, to their credit, but that early try by Tommy Gleeson put us on our way and we never looked like losing after that.'

'What about next season then 'Arold? D'you reckon there'll be a league?'

Harold studied for a moment and took a swig of beer before replying. 'I really don't know Norman. The Northern Union haven't made a decision yet but to be honest I can't see it myself. I don't think there will be another league until the war's over. That's why I was so desperate to get the four trophies this year.'

'Their calling you the Empire Team of All the Talents aren't they.'

'Aye, that's quite a complement isn't it and it recognises how we've brought players together from all over the Empire.'

Norman drained his pint and stood up 'Any road it's my shout, same again 'Arold?'

'Why not, the season's over so I can let myself go a bit can't I.'

Harold's prediction of the league programme being suspended until after the war turned out to be correct. By the time the war was over Harold would have tried his hand at a couple of other sports, one in particular with great success[21].

APPENDIX A – TOUR PROGRAMME

TOUR PROGRAMME, TEAMS AND RESULTS

DATE	OPPONENT / VENUE	TEAM/SCORERS	SCORE
6th June	METROPOLIS SCG	Wood, Robinson, Jenkins, Davies, Williams, Rogers, Prosser, Clampitt, Roman, Jarman, Holland, Smales, Guerin **Tries:** Holland, Prosser. **Goals:** Rogers, Guerin	10 – 38
8th June	NEW SOUTH WALES SCG	Thomas, Davies, Wagstaff, Jenkins, Moorhouse, Hall, Rogers, Coldrick, Clark, Johnson, Jarman, Holland, Chilcott **Try:** Wagstaff	3 – 11
13th June	QUEENSLAND BRISBANE	Thomas, Williams, Wagstaff, Davies, Francis, Smith, O'Garra, Guerin, Clark, Longstaff, Ramsdale, Smales, Chilcott **Tries:** Williams (2), Francis(2). **Goals:** Guerin (2), Thomas	18 – 10
17th June	IPSWICH	Jarman, Moorhouse, Wagstaff, Hall, Francis, Smith, Prosser, Clampitt, Roman, Coldrick, Longstaff, Holland, Johnson **Tries:** Francis (5), Moorhouse (3), Wagstaff (2), Johnson. **Goals:** Wagstaff (4), Jarman, Johnson	45 – 8

20th June	QUEENSLAND BRISBANE	Thomas, Williams, Wagstaff, Jenkins, Moorhouse, Hall, Rogers, Coldrick, Clark, Longstaff, Ramsdale, Jarman, Chilcott **Tries:** Moorhouse (2), Wagstaff, Hall, Rogers, Coldrick. **Goals:** Thomas, Longstaff.	22 – 8
24th June	NEWCASTLE	Wood, Francis, Wagstaff, Davies, Robinson, Smith, O'Garra, Roman, Clampitt, Guerin, Holland, Smales, Johnson **Tries:** Wagstaff (2), Davies, Robinson, Smith, O'Garra, Holland, Smales, Johnson. **Goals:** Wood (4)	35 – 18
27th June	AUSTRALIA Royal Agricultural Ground	Jarman, Robinson, Jenkins, Wagstaff, Moorhouse, Hall, Smith, Holland, Coldrick, Ramsdale, Chilcott, Longstaff, Clark **Tries:** Moorhouse (2), Robinson, Holland, Clark. **Goals:** Robinson (2), Longstaff (2)	23 – 5
29th June	AUSTRALIA SCG	Thomas, Williams, Wagstaff, Hall, Robinson, Rogers, Smith, Jarman, Ramsdale, Coldrick, Holland, Clark, Chilcott **Try:** Coldrick. **Goals:** Rogers (2)	7 – 12
2nd July	WESTERN DISTRICTS Bathurst	Wood, Williams, Hall, Davies, O'Garra, Prosser, Rogers, Roman, Clampitt, Guerin, Smales, Jarman, John-	42 – 3

		son. **Tries:** Hall (3), Davies (2), O'Garra (2), Johnson (2), Williams. **Goals:** Wood (2), Guerin (2), Rogers, Johnson	
4th July	AUSTRALIA SCG	Wood, Williams, Wagstaff, Hall, Davies, Prosser, Smith, Chilcott, Ramsdale, Coldrick, Holland, Clark, Johnson **Tries:** Davies, Johnson. **Goals:** Wood (4)	14 – 6
11th July	WELLINGTON	Thomas, Sam Houghton, Hall, Davies, O'Garra, Prosser, Smith, Guerin, Jarman, Chilcott, Smales, Roman, Clampitt **Tries:** Thomas, Houghton, Hall, Chilcott. **Goal:** Guerin	14 – 7
18th July	HAWKES BAY Napier	Thomas, Moorhouse, Wagstaff, Davies, O'Garra, Prosser, Smith, Roman, Clampitt, Johnson, Guerin, Jarman, Holland **Tries:** Davies (3), Wagstaff (2), Jarman. **Goals:** Guerin (5), Thomas	30 -7
23rd July	TARANAKI Eltham	Thomas, O'Garra, Wagstaff, Hall, Moorhouse, Prosser, Smith, Jarman, Roman, Clampitt, Guerin **Tries:** Moorhouse (5), O'Garra (2), Wagstaff, Hall, Smith, Roman. **Goals:** Guerin (5)	43 – 11
25th July	AUCKLAND	Wood, Moorhouse, Hall, Jenkins, Davies, Rogers, Smith, Rams-	34 -12

		dale, Johnson, Chilcott, Longstaff, Coldrick, Holland **Tries:** Moorhouse (2), Hall, Jenkins, Rogers, Ramsdale, Coldrick, Holland. **Goals:** Wood (5)	
30th July	WANGANUI	Wood, Moorhouse, Wagstaff, Jenkins, Davies, O'Garra, Prosser, Coldrick, Ramsdale, Longstaff, Guerin, Clampitt, Roman. **Tries:** Jenkins (3), Moorhouse (2), Wagstaff (2), Prosser (2), Longstaff (2), Guerin, Clampitt. **Goals:** Wood (9)	57 – 12
1st August	NEW ZEALAND Auckland	Wood, Davies, Jenkins, Wagstaff, Moorhouse, Hall, Smith, Holland, Coldrick, Ramsdale, Longstaff, Johnson, Clampitt. **Tries:** Moorhouse (2), Davies, Johnson. **Goals:** Wood (2)	16 – 13
15th August	NEW SOUTH WALES Melbourne CG	Wood, Moorhouse, Wagstaff, Jenkins, Davies, Hall, Rogers, Coldrick, Clampitt, Ramsdale, Longstaff, Chilcott, Johnson **Tries:** Moorhouse, Jenkins, Coldrick. **Goals:** Wood (6)	21 – 15
		TOTALS	434 – 196

Footnote: The Northern Union played an exhibition match in Adelaide against a South Australia select team on 24th May 1914, which they won by 101 points to nil, but this was not considered a first class match.

APPENDIX B – PLAYING RECORDS

PLAYING RECORDS

NAME / CLUB	APPEARANCES (TESTS)	TRIES SCORED	GOALS SCORED	POINTS SCORED
ENGLISH PLAYERS				
JIM CLAMPITT – Broughton Rangers	10(1)	1		3
DOUGLAS CLARK – Huddersfield	6 (3)	1		3
JOE GUERIN – Hunslet	8	1	15	33
BILLY HALL – Oldham	12 (4)	7		21
DAVE HOLLAND – Oldham	9 (4)	4		12
BILLY JARMAN – Leeds	10 (2)	1	1	5
'CHIC' JOHNSON -Widnes	9 (2)	5	2	19
FRED LONGSTAFF – Huddersfield	8 (2)	2	4	14
STAN MOORHOUSE – Huddersfield	10 (2)	19		57
JACK O'GARRA – Widnes	7	5		15
DICK RAMSDALE – Wigan	9 (4)	1		3
JACK ROBINSON – Rochdale Hornets	4 (2)	2	2	10
'RATTLER' ROMAN – Rochdale Hornets	7	1		3
JOHN SMALES – Hunslet	6	1		3
FRED SMITH – Hunslet	10 (4)	2		6
HAROLD WAGSTAFF (capt) Huddersfield	13 (4)	11	4	41
ALF WOOD – Oldham	8 (2)		32	64
WELSH PLAYERS				
JACK CHILCOTT – Huddersfield	9 (3)	1		3
PERCY COLDRICK – Wigan	10 (4)	4		12
WILLIE DAVIES – Leeds (vice-captain)	10 (2)	9		27
ALF FRANCIS – Hull	3	7		21
BERT JENKINS – Wigan	8 (2)	5		15
STUART PROSSER – Halifax	8 (1)	3		9
JOHNNY ROGERS – Huddersfield	7 (1)	2	4	14
GWYN THOMAS – Wigan	7 (1)	1	3	9
FRANK WILLIAMS – Halifax	6 (2)	3		9
GUEST APPEARANCE				
SAM HOUGHTON – Napier NZ	1	1		3
TOTALS		**100**	**67**	**434**

NOTES

[1] The official name of the team was the Northern Union but many of the newspapers and other officials would refer to the team as England.

[2] There were in fact 9 Welshmen in the squad of 26.

[3] If the Northern Union had won the second test they would have an unassailable lead of 2 test to nil with only one test remaining.

[4] Lakin' – northern slang for playing.

[5] Touch and pass is a non contact game of rugby where a player simply has to be touched to be regarded as tackled. The game would restart when the 'tackled' player touches his foot with the ball and passes it to a team-mate. Sometimes referred to as 'Touch Rugby'.

[6] The Yorkshire version of the word father was spoken with a very short 'a' to rhyme with gather.

[7] 'sen' is the Yorkshire slang for self, so 'sit yourself down' would be 'sit the sen down'. Similarly 'me'sen' would mean myself

[8] Nobbut – Yorkshire slang for 'only'

[9] Broughton Rangers were founder members and one of the leading sides in the Northern Union based in Salford. They later became Belle Vue Rangers, eventually they folded in 1955

[10] Si'thee Yorkshire slang for see you

[11] A sovereign was £1/1 shilling (£1.05p). Therefore the approximate income value of 5 sovereigns would be £588 in 2020.

[12] Back home – at this time England was often referred to as 'Back Home' or the 'Old Country' by people living in the colonies.

[13] December 6th 1905, Cardiff Arms Park, Wales 3 NZ 0

[14] 25 shillings would be £1 and 5 shillings (£1.25 in new money) and was winning pay for a back. Payment for a loss or draw was 10 shillings (50p). Forwards were paid less just £1 for a win and 7 shillings and 6 pence (37.5p) for a draw or defeat.

[15] 'bob' – slang word for a shilling (5p).

[16] Jack Bartholomew was in fact the uncle of Eric Morecambe whose real name was also Bartholomew.

[17] The Yorkshire League was not a separate competition but was run alongside the championship. Points gained in matches against other Yorkshire sides were accumulated and the team with the most points was crowned champions. The Lancashire League was decided in a similar manner.

[18] A Smoke Social was a peculiarly Australasian event. It was a strictly men only event and, as the name suggests, tobacco smoking and social chat was the main focus of the event but a formal dinner would often also form part of the event.

[19] The five games played in Sydney had a total attendance of 215,255 and receipts of £11,764

[20] The overall gross receipts for the tour were just under £16,000. The Northern Union share would be just under £10,000.

[21] Harold Wagstaff, along with several Northern Union stars would be picked to represent the Army Service Corps at Grove Park, London where they won all but one of their games scoring 1,110 points and conceding only 41. His Huddersfield colleagues Douglas Clark, Ben Gronow and Albert Rosenfeld all featured in the side. When asked what the secret of the Grove Park team's success was, Harold replied 'We simply played Northern Union football under Rugby Union rules'.

Printed in Great Britain
by Amazon